Portraits of *Faith*

the biography of

Liz Lemon Swindle

written by Susan Easton Black

Portraits of *Faith*

the biography of Liz Lemon Swindle

CFI
An Imprint of Cedar Fort, Inc.
Springville, Utah

ISBN 13: 978-1-4621-4269-9

Published by CFI, an imprint of Cedar Fort, Inc.
2373 W. 700 S., Springville, UT 84663
Distributed by Cedar Fort, Inc., www.cedarfort.com

THE LIBRARY OF CONGRESS HAS CATALOGED THE HARDBACK EDITION AS FOLLOWS:

Names: Black, Susan Easton, author.
Title: Portraits of faith : the biography of Liz Lemon Swindle / Susan Easton Black.
Description: Springville, Utah : CFI, an imprint of Cedar Fort, Inc., [2017] | Includes bibliographical references and index.
Identifiers: LCCN 2016054073 (print) | LCCN 2016055752 (ebook) | ISBN 9781462119523 (perfect bound : alk. paper) | ISBN 9781462127269 (epub, pdf, mobi)
Subjects: LCSH: Swindle, Liz Lemon, 1953- | Mormon women--Biography. | Mormon artists--Utah--Biography.
Classification: LCC BX8695.S95 B53 2017 (print) | LCC BX8695.S95 (ebook) | DDC 289.3092 [B] --dc23
LC record available at https://lccn.loc.gov/2016054073

Cover design by Kinsey Beckett

Edited and typeset by Rebecca Bird

Printed in the United States of America

10 9 8 7 6 5 4 3 2 1

Printed on acid-free paper

Contents

Introduction

At BYU's Education Week, customers waited anxiously to purchase a painting by Liz Lemon Swindle and to catch a glimpse of one of the most famous LDS artists of our time. What most in the crowd didn't realize is that the popularity of Liz's art is not just a Utah County phenomenon. Liz has captured a worldwide Christian audience. At art shows with Catholics, Baptists, and other Christian faiths, good people hoping to purchase a painting of Jesus Christ to display in their homes surround Liz. Liz is up front about being a Mormon, with a pioneer heritage that runs deep. Some say she wears her religion on her sleeve.

Many are curious about the life of Liz Lemon Swindle and the events that led to her becoming a classical realist artist. When Liz is slow to respond, those who fancy themselves in the know speak of her being reared in The Avenues of Salt Lake City, attending East High School, and having parents who placed a silver paintbrush in her hand and proudly announced, "Our daughter will one day paint the Restoration and the life of Christ. She is a Rembrandt in the making." They picture Liz hobnobbing with the societal even philanthropic crowds who cater to her every whim. Others speak of Liz attending the most prestigious art schools in the nation before traveling to Europe to study the works of old masters like Leonardo da Vinci and Michelangelo.

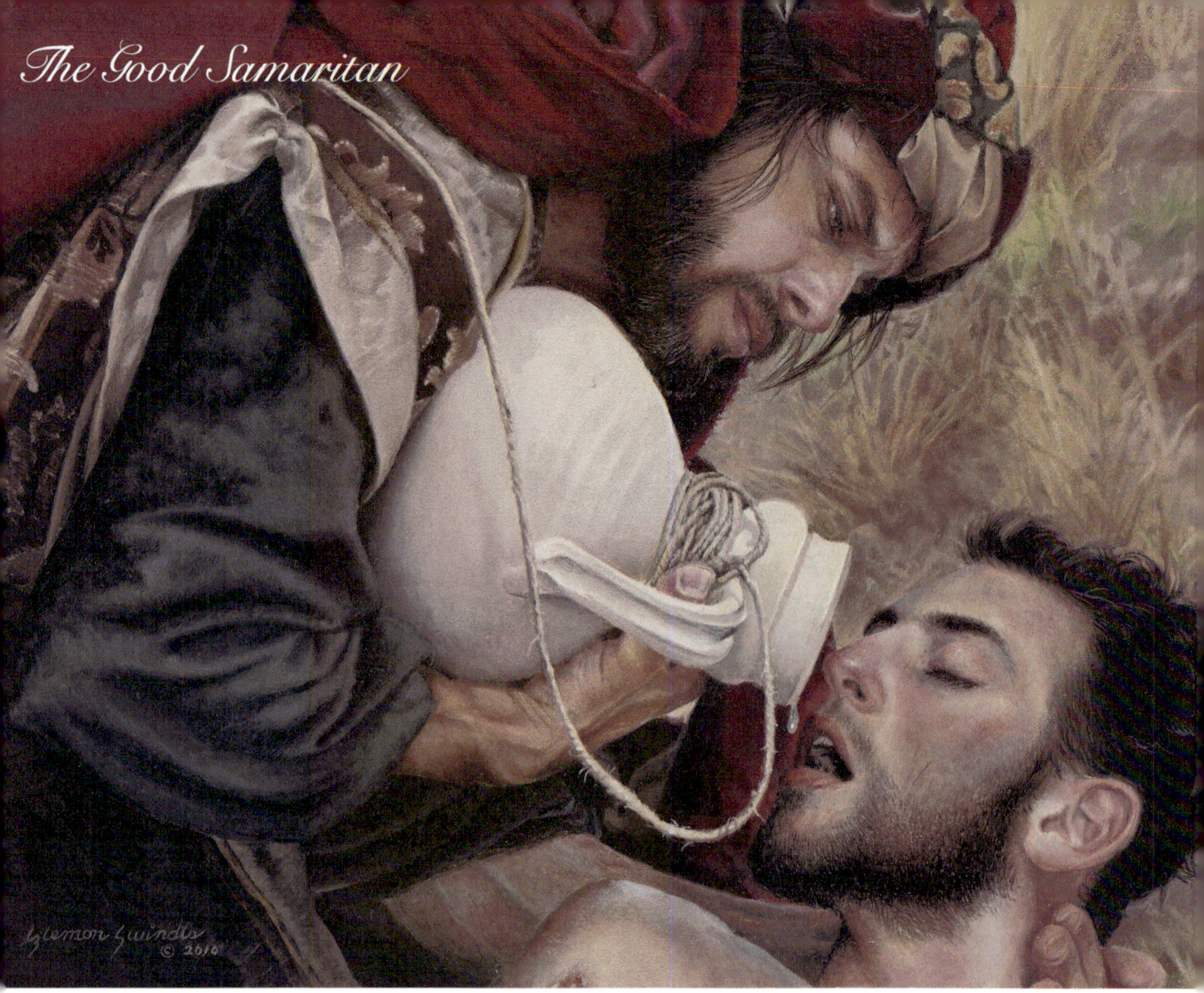

The Good Samaritan

If these theories were true, the life of Liz Lemon Swindle would be wonderful, if not predictable. Each step in her journey would've been expected and lined with applause. Paint smudges and personal difficulties, if there were any, would be explained away as mere stepping-stones to greater triumphs.

However, the story of Liz Lemon Swindle has a humble beginning. Liz's father, a bookkeeper for a rural cannery, suffered from progressive deafness and her mother and siblings had learning disabilities. Yet it was her father, Elmer R. Matthews, who gave Liz the first of many sketch pads—glossy tomato can labels from the Perry Cannery. Her father was never Liz's art tutor or mentor, but on Sunday afternoons he would say, "Let's sit down and draw."

As Liz drew on the backside of the labels, Elmer put a record on the phonograph and sat next to her to watch the artistic rendering unfold.

The journey of Liz Lemon Swindle from drawing on can labels to working as a set painter at the Osmond Studios to being sent a papal blessing from the Pope in Rome is a story not easily dismissed, for it is a journey that has taken Liz and her religious art around the world. Her original paintings and numbered prints are sold in exclusive art galleries from California to Connecticut. Her works have been featured on covers of the *Ensign*, evangelical magazines, and on personal Christmas cards of an archbishop of the Catholic Church.

Liz's contribution to Christian art and the Latter-day Saint faith stands unprecedented with her paintings spanning from the Old Testament to the Doctrine and Covenants. She has painted over forty artistic renderings on the life of Joseph Smith and over eighty renderings on the life and teachings of Jesus Christ, not to mention countless sketches on both subject matters. Her paintings have been exhibited in LDS Visitors' Centers across the nation, motion picture studios, and even on a White House Christmas card.

Portraits of Faith: The Biography of Liz Lemon Swindle is the story of a woman who has become one of the most acclaimed Latter-day Saint artists of our time. Her story is not one of ease, but of faith in the Lord. Her dogged determination has blessed millions through her poignant religious art.

Family Life in Perry

The story of Liz Lemon Swindle begins in Perry, Utah, where cattle, peach orchards, and tomato crops outnumbered residents, and the Perry cannery and Maddox Ranch House restaurant were the prominent town landmarks. Her childhood was not like those of other young girls growing up in a tranquil rural setting because her parents were anything but ordinary. Some say they were extraordinary.

At age ten, Elmer announced to his parents, both British immigrants, "I'm not going to church anymore." Elmer's parents were okay with his decision because church attendance was not a high priority for them or others residing in the mining town of Castle Dale in eastern Utah. On that particular Sabbath day, Elmer and his friend filled a makeshift Bunsen burner with fuel that quickly caught fire. In the panic and chaos that ensued, Elmer was convinced his predicament was a direct message from God that he should've gone to church. Elmer made a promise to the Lord that if He would put out the fire, Elmer would never miss church again. Elmer kept that promise. In his mind, there was no excuse good enough to deny the Lord His day. As a result, watching Sunday televised broadcasts of *The Wonderful World of Disney*, *The Ed Sullivan Show*, *The Wizard of Oz*, and the Beatles were never part of Liz's childhood. However, an emergency Sunday visit to the doctor was—but only after sacrament meeting was over.

"Being the daughter of a religious fanatic," Liz says, "wasn't all bad." Her father's association and friendship with many Church leaders gave Liz needed insight into his unwavering devotion. As she matured, Liz realized this was a choice gift her father had given to her. Although Liz's parents were far from ordinary, their influence made Liz the person she is today.

Elmer Matthews

Elmer, though slight of frame at only 5'6", was one of the fortunate young men to survive the devastating 1918 flu epidemic that took the lives of 21.5 million people around the world. Though he survived the flu, it left him with a 75 percent hearing loss. Before the illness, Elmer dreamed of becoming a teacher and had graduated from the Brigham Young Academy in Provo. He learned to adapt to his impairment by reading lips and using sign language. Unfortunately, most folks in rural Perry still found it difficult to converse with him. By the time Liz was born in 1953 at the Cooley Memorial Hospital in Brigham City, fifty-two-year-old Elmer had slightly improved his hearing by use of a hearing aid.

Although most people suffering from hearing loss develop speech problems, Elmer's speech and diction remained perfect. Yet too often Sunday fast and testimony meetings proved difficult for Liz. Elmer's hearing aid reacted to the microphone with a piercing screech, sending Liz under the pew—figuratively speaking. It was hard for Liz to hear laughter coming from the back of the chapel as her father expressed the tender feelings of his heart. Sadly, Liz spent far too much time wishing her father wouldn't follow the promptings of the Spirit that compelled him to bear his testimony. At the time, Liz cared more about the acceptance of peers rather than her father's expression of love for his Heavenly Father. Today Liz would give her all to hear her father's unequivocal testimony of Jesus Christ and the Restoration of the gospel. "My heart longs to hear that screech one more time," Liz says.

The hearing impairment might have stopped most young men from serving an LDS mission, but not Elmer. At a time when other youth felt strangled by what they perceived as constraints of The Church of Jesus Christ of

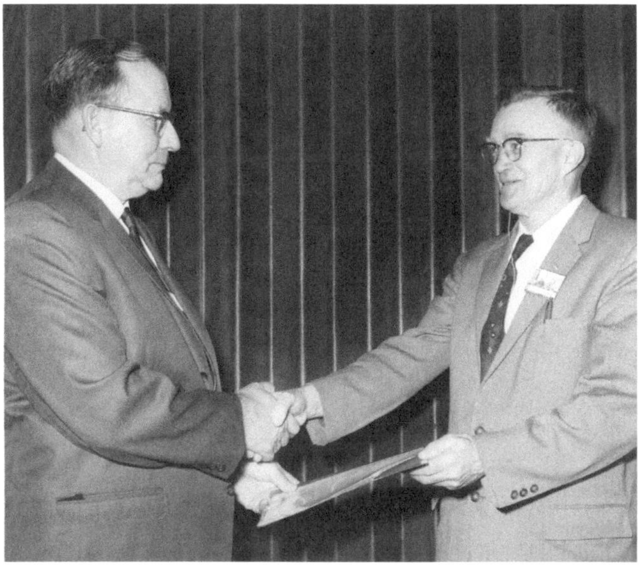

Elmer Matthews, pictured on the right.

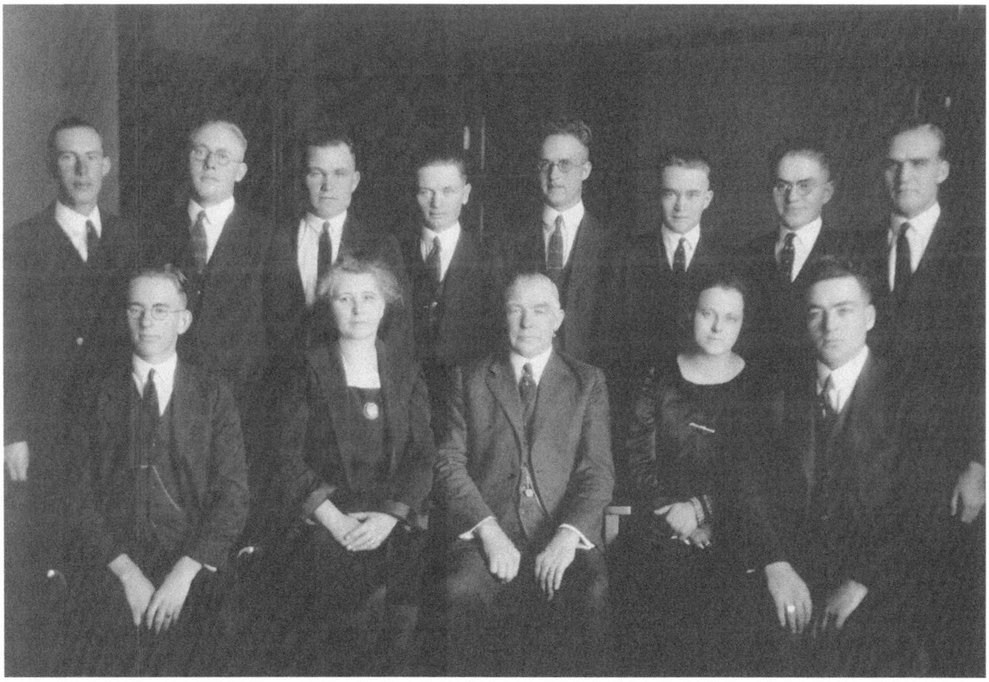

Elmer Matthews's mission photo. Elmer Matthews is second from the right on the back row and Harold B. Lee is on the far right on the front row.

Latter-day Saints, Elmer wanted to reach out and share the Restoration message. At age nineteen he accepted a mission call to the Western States, which meant saying goodbye to his family and the love of his life—a young woman named Annie from eastern Utah. Partway through his three-year mission, Elmer received a "Dear John letter" from Annie. He was devastated. Fellow missionaries tried to reassure him that there would be other women beating down his door, but the gestures of love and friendship had little effect on Elmer.

Among the missionaries who consoled young Elmer was Harold B. Lee. Elder Lee proved not only a good friend to Elmer in the mission field, but also an exceptional friend to him throughout his life. At harvest season each year Elmer took bushels of homegrown peaches, cherries, apples, and tomatoes to Elder Lee of the Quorum of the Twelve in Salt Lake City. Liz recalls accompanying her father on many visits to the home of Elder Lee. Of particular interest to Liz was a vase of five, ten, and twenty dollar bills shaped like fans, meant to look like flowers, resting atop a baby grand piano. When asked why she focused on the money, Liz replied, "I seldom saw money in my home—not even loose change."

On Elmer's harvest runs was a stop at the home of President David O. McKay. Bushels of fruits and vegetables were presented to the McKays in exchange for an afternoon with swings, horses, and home-baked cookies. Liz thought President McKay and his wife were two of the kindest people she had ever met. As a very young child, Liz was convinced that President McKay was Santa Claus because of his stark white hair.

Elmer's honesty and work ethic landed him the position of general manager in the Perry Canning company when the United States entered World War II. Unable to serve in the military due to his hearing loss, Elmer was called upon to keep the company afloat while most of the male employees were fighting in the war abroad. As Elmer thought about how to keep the cannery going, he concluded that one answer was to start a night shift and invite women to take the place of their husbands and sort the produce that moved slowly along the conveyor belts. Most of the women who expressed interest in working at the cannery didn't have transportation. To solve the problem Elmer drove his "woody" station wagon around Box Elder County, picking the women up before their shifts and taking them home when their shifts ended.

Marie Wight

One woman who depended on Elmer for transportation to the cannery was Marie Wight. Marie stood 5'2" in height. At the time of her employment, twenty-eight-year-old Marie was viewed as a spinster with a learning disability. She recognized her limitations. Marie had grown frustrated in the school setting and dropped out of high school. Liz was told her mother's disability was the result of a bee sting, but Liz never believed it.

By age forty-eight Elmer had never married. With the passing of his father, he cared for his mother until her death. Many saw this as Elmer sacrificing his life for his mother, but he never saw it as a sacrifice. He simply loved his parents and honored them. But there was sorrow in his life. With each passing year, Elmer could see his hope of ever marrying and having a family growing dim.

At the cannery, Marie Wight was assigned to sort peaches with other women on the conveyor belt. She was successful at performing the task and was invited to be the "floor-lady," managing other women who sorted fruit passing along the belt. Liz thinks the advancement had much to do with the attention of her father. Elmer admitted to himself that he had feelings for Marie even though his mother strongly objected. As Elmer drove the women home from the cannery, he planned the route so that Marie was the last worker dropped off each night.

Turning to his trusted confidant Harold B. Lee, Elmer arranged a time when he could talk with the Apostle about the woman working at the cannery. During their conversation Elder Lee reminded Elmer that he wasn't getting any younger and advised him to marry. At the conclusion of their conversation Elder Lee said, "I would like to meet this woman." When told of Elmer's meeting with Elder Lee, Marie arranged her affairs to go to Salt Lake City to

CHURCH OF JESUS CHRIST OF LATTER DAY SAINTS
THE COUNCIL OF THE TWELVE
47 E. SOUTH TEMPLE STREET
SALT LAKE CITY, UTAH

December 10, 1947

Mr. Elmer Matthews
c/o Perry Canning Company
R. F. D. No. 2
Brigham City, Utah

Dear Elmer:

I have what I am pleased to call "your report of progress" on the assignment I gave you two years ago to find a wife. Of course I will be happy to visit with you whenever you find it convenient. I think you are in the same position that some girls are when they pass the usual age for marriage - they become too particular and rigid in their requirements for a companion and sometimes allow little differences to blind them to the greater potentialities. I think, if I were you, I would not be greatly concerned about the difference in your age and that of Marie. If she has the basic qualities I am sure your living together will lend to each other the inspiration necessary to make congenial all other minor differences. I don't think you can expect the Lord to come down and give you a separate dispensation and tell you whether Marie is the right girl or not, but he will give you the right to impressions as to whether she would provide that feeling of comradship and ability to work in husband-wife team in meeting adversity, solving problems, rearing a family, and in enduring all necessary privations to achieve a desired goal.

You certainly are not an old man at 46-47; in fact, one would guess you to be ten or more years younger than that. You need to have some further responsibilities as a husband and father in order to make you look your age. There is another thing to be remembered - that a pretty face and figure do not guarantee a beautiful soul. Sometimes those who are superficially pretty, when better known, lose their charm, and some of those passed by in a foolish man's search, as a honey bee would search for the sweet nectar from flower to flower, oftimes prove to be the enduring gold that only needs but the refining experience of love and appreciation from a worthy husband. I wouldn't be surprised if your little English mother's opinion of this girl might be rather helpful.

Assuring you always of my interest in your welfare and pleasure in seeing you any time you can find it convenient, I am

Faithfully your brother,

Harold B. Lee

Harold B. Lee

c

meet with the Apostle. After their cordial meeting, Elder Lee sent a letter to Elmer advising him to marry Marie Wight.

The Marriage of Elmer and Marie

The marriage of Elmer and Marie was epic in the little town of Perry. Things were said and opinions were formed about the whys of such a marriage, but Elmer loved Marie and could see beyond what others saw and Marie simply adored Elmer. Their marriage was happy—filled with love and kindness.

Elmer's love for the Lord spilled over into all aspects of his life, including his marriage. In choosing an eternal partner he asked for advice from one of the Lord's chosen Apostles and followed the advice. One of Liz's fondest memories was watching her parents dance to the music of *The Lawrence Welk Show* on television every Saturday night. "My parents were sometimes awkward, but they were always wonderful," Liz says.

Elmer had boundless energy. He would get up every morning before five o'clock to change pipes on his forty-acre farm and attend to the chores of farm life. From eight to five he worked at the cannery with the exception of lunchtime. At noon, he came home, ate lunch, and watched two soap operas—*One Life to Live* and *The Edge of Night*—on a small black-and-white television set. When he returned from work in the late afternoon, Elmer would eat dinner and go outside to work on the farm until daylight was gone. Liz credits her strong work ethic and disdain for soap operas to the example of her father.

Occasionally Elmer would travel to San Francisco on cannery business and meet with executives of Safeway. On one occasion when the family was able to go with him, Liz remembers watching from the car window as her father drove away from the city. The lit windows of a beautiful mansion had a story to tell her. The windows were bright with yellows and oranges that stood out against the deep purples and blues of the sky at dusk. Years later Liz learned that artistic principles were at work that evening. The colors were opposites on the color wheel. Often when opposite colors are placed next to each other, they create a sense of movement as if they are coming to life. They

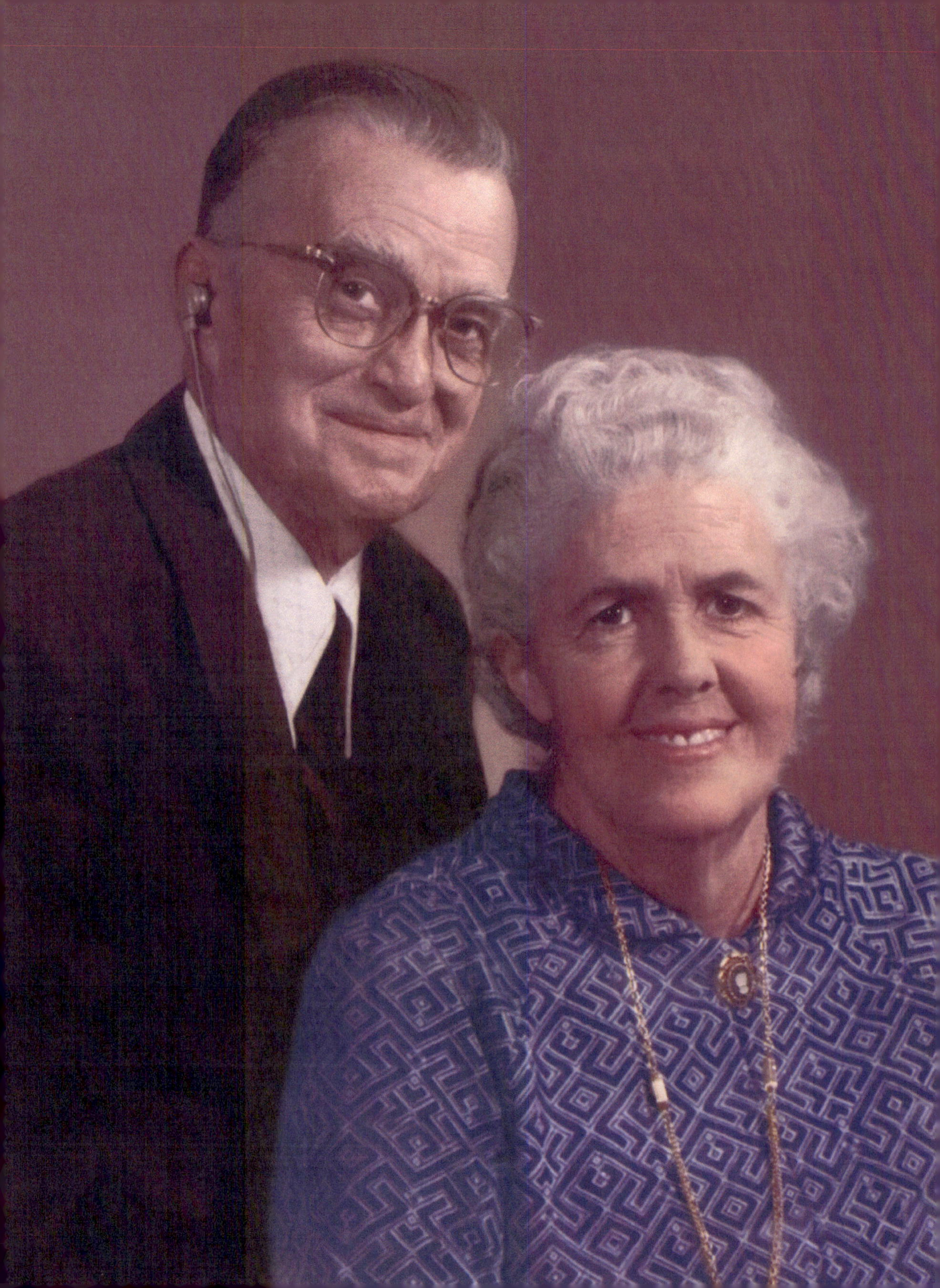

seem to complete each other. Liz looks back on the lives of her parents and sees the metaphor—her father was orange and her mother blue.

Liz's mother never worked outside the home after she married Elmer. "One of the best parts of my childhood was knowing when I got home, Mom would be there," Liz says. But despite being at home with her children, Marie never learned to drive a car, so Liz had to wait for her father to drive her any place she wanted to go. Going to a department store was especially difficult for Liz. It meant that either her father accompanied her on shopping sprees or her father insisted her mother and siblings come along. Elmer was more than happy to drop off Liz and her siblings at the JCPenney store on Main Street in Brigham City. After shopping and walking four miles back to her home, Liz learned to space shopping excursions far apart.

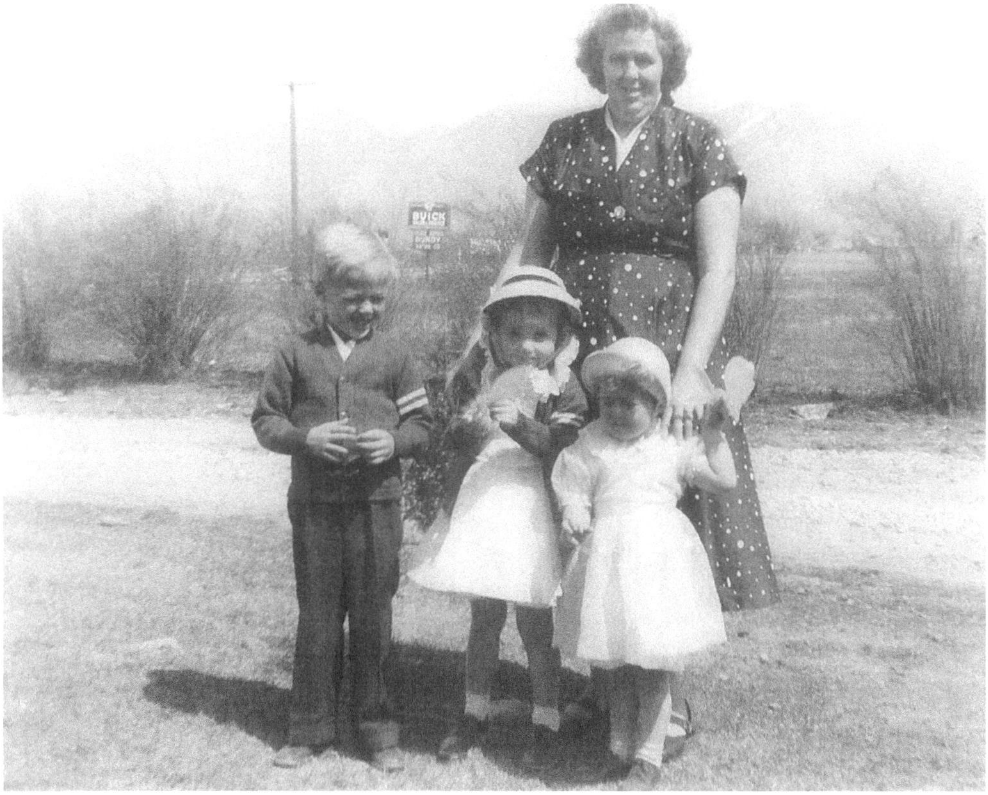

Concerning dresses, Elmer and Marie's rule was "the hemline must cover the knees"—a very unpopular style at that time. The miniskirt was the favorite style for teenage girls in Perry. Knowing her parents would never agree to such a purchase, Liz came up with a plan. She'd catch the school bus in the morning in the approved dress. In about fifteen minutes Liz could hem her skirt to a length that would please even the model Twiggy. At the end of the school day Liz had roughly twenty-five minutes to take out the hem before the school bus stopped near her home.

Elmer and Marie had four children—the first, a son named Charles, known as Charlie, and three daughters, Anne Marie, Elizabeth, and Martha. Liz felt obliged to protect her sisters and even her older brother from bullies at school and church. This sense of obligation was not without inner struggles. On one level Liz was protecting her siblings and on another, embarrassed by their actions. She was always a little different from her siblings, a gap that widened over time as Liz set goals. Although her father put away college funds for each child, Liz was the only one to use the funds.

The Young Liz

At a very young age, Liz mistakenly felt she was not pretty. Perhaps to compensate, she sketched princesses wearing flowing dresses and crowns. Her drawings caught the attention of Eva Young, the first and second grade teacher at Perry Elementary. Mrs. Young called Elmer one day in frustration to say, "All Liz wants to do is draw. She draws on desks, walls, papers, and just about anything she can find." Before Liz could become a graffiti artist, Elmer intervened by bringing home discarded tomato can labels from the cannery and encouraged Liz to draw on the backside of the labels. The labels had a glossy finish, not exactly the right paper for a budding artist. Not knowing the difference between good paper and poor paper, Liz was excited and grateful for the labels. As far as art pencils, they were found in the junk drawer or atop her father's desk—a simple #2 pencil was perfect.

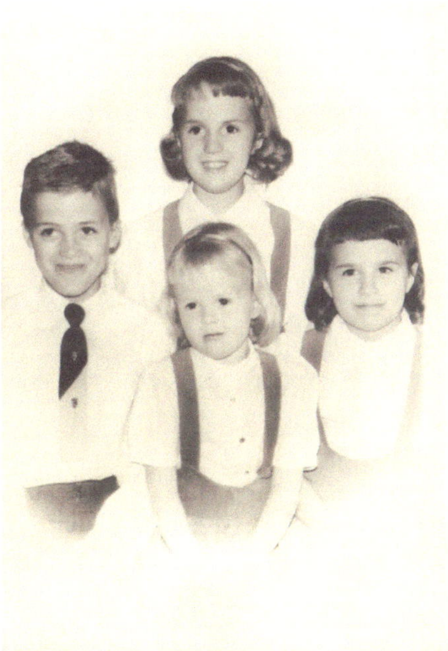

Dick and Jane readers, Norman Rockwell paintings in the *Saturday Evening Post*, and Breck Shampoo advertisements were her inspiration. Liz was drawn to fine detail, like the iconic redheaded children in Norman Rockwell paintings, the doll that Spot chewed up in the *Dick and Jane* books, and the shiny single strands of hair in the Breck Shampoo advertisements. Although Rockwell never knew he was her mentor, young Liz thought his art was the best. She worked hard to draw faces with emotion like the expressions found in Rockwell's paintings. Regardless of the subject matter or skill level of Liz's artistic renderings, Elmer taped her creations to the refrigerator for what he termed "a private showing."

In second grade, Liz won a blue ribbon at the county fair for her drawing of Smokey Bear. This was her first art award, but certainly not her last. Liz was pleased with the recognition, but some of her friends were not. When complimented on her extraordinary talent, she would invariably hear a friend and even an adult whisper, "That's just one of the Matthews." Such character assassination hurt and angered Liz. It led her to say, "One day I'll show them." She was ready to fight and stand up for herself, her siblings, and her talent. Her father would often tell her that one day she may have to take care of her siblings. Liz promised herself and the Lord that she would work hard and learn all about art so she could take care of her family.

When it came to the Church, Liz was confused by leaders and teachers alike who taught of Christ but often didn't act Christlike. They taught that Heavenly Father and Jesus loved everyone and we should do the same. Liz couldn't understand why the leaders and teachers said disparaging things about her and her family that contradicted what they taught. Then there were the children, who were quick to give the right answers but just as quick to be cruel to her brother and sisters. Liz never doubted whether the LDS Church was true, but she often asked herself why the Church produced such "two-faced saints."

It was especially tough for Liz in Primary, for there she not only witnessed bullying but was also conscious of the wide economic gap between herself and the other children. For example, the day Liz saw a young girl holding a cute purse, she wanted a cute purse too. "I knew my father would never allow his hard earned money to be spent on such frivolity," Liz recalls. "His famous line was 'Can't afford it.'" Liz also struggled with the pictures of Jesus in her family Bible, such as the painting of him whipping the money changers from of the temple. She asked herself, "How can I embrace his love when the pictures evoke so much fear?"

Junior High and High School

In junior high, Liz was very aware of who was popular and who was not. In Perry, the popular crowd were those living in the "subdivision" and wearing cute clothes. Liz recalls, "At school, the teenage girls in the group were tiny and looked like Marie Osmond. They wore make-up, mini-skirts, and matching shoes." Liz pled with her father for money to purchase make-up and stylish clothes. "Can't afford it," Elmer would say, characteristically. He was not interested in whether his talented daughter belonged to the popular group or wore the latest fashion trend.

Knowing her father wouldn't change his stance, Liz took a sewing class and learned how to make her own patterns and sew her own clothes. The skill came easy, perhaps because she had designed and sewed so many clothes for her Barbie Dolls. The only difference between Barbie dresses and her own was the size of the fabric. Liz picked cherries for her father and worked at her cousin Jay Matthews' fruit stand to earn money to purchase fabric. To subsidize these after-school jobs, Liz painted designs on shoes, T-shirts, and ties, which she sold to friends and by word of mouth. Although the popular crowd never embraced Liz, they bragged about owning a pair of shoes she painted.

Liz preferred to be doing something rather than sitting still and watching television. But on Thursday nights, when her parents were away from home serving as missionary guides in the Brigham City Tabernacle, she watched *Bewitched* because the leading character, Samantha, wore cute clothes. Watching television on Saturday nights was a family affair. The weekly routine was *The Lawrence Welk Show* followed by *The Carol Burnett Show* and *Gunsmoke* and then it was time for bed. Occasionally Liz sneaked a peek at

American Bandstand on Saturday mornings to catch the latest dance moves and popular bands, but Saturdays were the day her family got ready for Sunday so her dance moves suffered.

As for movies, hands down Liz's favorite was *Follow Me Boys*, starring teenage heartthrob Kurt Russell. Liz was in love with Russell from the moment he appeared on the silver screen. She purchased a movie magazine with his picture on the cover so that she could draw his face again and again. By age thirteen Liz knew she would one day be Mrs. Kurt Russell. As her father was taping yet another sketch of the movie star to the refrigerator door, he said, "Oh, that's lovely, dear, but maybe you could draw prophets like David O. McKay too."

To appease her father, Liz drew a portrait of Elder Harold B. Lee. Elmer was so pleased with her drawing that he folded the portrait—with no idea about the value of art—and sent it to Elder Lee. Liz is certain her father sent the drawing to Elder Lee so that she would stop painting Kurt Russell. Elder Lee wrote a letter to Liz thanking her for the lovely portrait, advising her to use her talent wisely, and assuring her that she had the gift to become an artist. He included a five dollar bill in the envelope with the recommendation that Liz buy art supplies. She bought mascara instead. Her father was not pleased. The little discretionary money in the household was not to be spent on make-up for his teenage daughter. Elmer strongly believed that he had a special responsibility to help shape the future of his talented daughter. To him that meant hiring Kay Peterson, an art teacher at the junior high, to help Liz advance in art, not indulging her in make-up so she could fit in with the popular crowd.

Under the tutelage of Kay Peterson, Liz won the prestigious Utah Conservation Soil Award for her drawing of trees. Liz's introduction to oil painting came from Peterson, an extraordinary teacher.

The Love of a Leader

Another extraordinary teacher was Jean Barnard, Liz's Laurel advisor. Sister Barnard was beautiful. She had money and class and was a prominent, well-respected civic leader in the community. Liz recalls Sister Barnard hosting a dinner party to teach etiquette and proper manners to the Laurels. Sister Barnard quickly learned that this social grace was a lifestyle many Laurels didn't want. Perry was a simple farming community and most girls wanted nothing more than to get married and raise a family. These were wonderful goals—goals that Liz also wanted. Yet Liz wanted more. She wanted to realize some of her other fondest dreams.

At this instructional party, one Laurel took too many trips to the food table. As diplomatically as Sister Barnard could, she took that occasion to teach the group about food etiquette. That was all this girl needed to take offense. She left the party with several other Laurels but not without giving this well-intentioned teacher a piece of her mind and not without biasing the rest of the Laurels against Sister Barnard. Most of the girls felt that Sister Barnard was conceited and not really interested in their lives beyond her calling, but Liz thought differently. To Liz, Sister Barnard was the most fascinating woman she had ever met and she didn't care if her motives were genuine or not. Liz would take those couple of hours every week if that's all there was.

It wasn't long before Sister Barnard saw the potential in this young misfit of a girl and loved her. From the beginning Sister Barnard took Liz under her wing and began a year of instruction that went far beyond that of a Young Women's leader. She taught Liz things her mother couldn't teach her, like social etiquette. She opened her home to Liz so that she could have parties and entertain friends. She taught her how to run a household and keep a clean house. She taught her to believe in her dreams. Until Sister Barnard took an interest in Liz, Elmer was the only person in Liz's life who believed in her total potential—not just in the arts, but as a daughter of God. Sister Barnard wasn't trying to fill the role of a mother, but that of a dear friend.

One experience Liz will never forget is the day her best friend Katie died, the last day of April 1970. Sister Barnard contacted Liz as soon as she heard of Katie's death and asked, "Did Katie commit suicide?" Liz responded with a resounding, "No!" Yet something inside wouldn't let Liz pass it off as hearsay.

Liz and Katie had been planning the "big date" for weeks. Liz was going with a cute boy in school and Katie was going with his friend. They were double dating to the Sadie Hawkins dance and both were excited—or at least Liz thought her best friend was excited about the dance. Katie had been quiet the last couple of days on the school bus. It was noticeable because Katie was never quiet. On April 30, Katie wasn't at school. When Liz arrived home that afternoon, her mother broke the news to her. "Katie is dead," she said, but the words didn't make any sense to Liz. "I couldn't take it in," Liz says. "I told my mother, 'She's just sick.'" Her mother said, "Katie's mother found her this morning on her bed at about ten o'clock."

Liz dropped her books and ran to Katie's house about a block away. She was met by Katie's sister and led into the living room where Katie's family was crying and talking in whispers—an unfamiliar site in the home. It was then Liz realized, "It must be true."

The days that followed were like a fog to Liz. The funeral was quiet. Liz thought to herself, "Katie would never like this. She would want noise and loud music. Why aren't they playing loud music for Katie?" Liz ended up going to the dance but doesn't remember much about it.

This wasn't the first time Liz faced the death of a close friend. When she was nine years old, her best friend, Arlene Egan, was hit by a car. That experience was surreal too. But with Katie's death Liz's walls went up. She now saw herself as a curse to anyone who'd venture a best friend relationship with her. Sister Barnard consoled Liz and tried to help her see Katie's death as an event, not a pattern of deaths that involved Liz. Although well intentioned, Sister Barnard was unsuccessful in convincing Liz that if she made a new best friend, the friend would not die.

Sister Barnard continued to encourage Liz to develop her talents. During her high school years, Liz responded to a magazine advertisement inviting contestants to sketch the picture that appeared in the magazine and send the sketch to an art institute. The winner of the contest was promised a full-tuition scholarship to a four-year college. Liz submitted her drawing to the art institute. In a few weeks she was notified of being a finalist and told that a representative from the art institute would be at a hotel in Brigham City to interview her. Liz shared the exciting news with Sister Barnard.

"Sister Barnard wanted to come with me," Liz recalls. "She planned to stay in the car while I went inside the hotel to meet with the art representative. But when we drove up to the hotel, Sister Barnard said, 'You're not going in there without me.' As it turned out the so-called art representative had nothing to do with art. He was smoking and his tie was loose. His shirt was so tight that it didn't even cover his stomach. Sister Barnard grabbed my hand and we both rushed out of his hotel room back to the car." That was the end of it except for some advice from Sister Barnard: "Always live your life so that when the Spirit speaks, you won't have to ask any questions." Liz says, "Jean Barnard magnified her calling as a teacher of young women. She will forever stand out in my mind as extraordinary and the perfect example of what a teacher should be."

High School Bragging Rights

Reflecting on her high school years, Liz is proudest of three accomplishments. First, Liz tried out for Rockettes, an elite all-girl drill team named after the famous Rockettes who performed at Radio City Hall on Broadway in New York. Liz made the drill team. The twenty-four-member team performed at high school sporting events, parades, and drill team competitions. Liz's excitement of being selected to be a Rockette went unchecked until she overheard the student body president-elect whisper, "She made Rockettes?" in disbelief. Although Liz never brushed off his comment, she marched with precision, kicked her legs to the beat, did splits with ease, tied wiglets to the back of her head, and had fun. She actually made the team twice—her sophomore and senior years. Unfortunately, being in Rockettes put a financial strain on her father. Liz couldn't make enough money at her after-school jobs to cover the costs of the Rockettes' uniforms, so dropping out was her only option in her sophomore year. But in her senior year Liz was back on the team, and in her words, "I had a blast!"

Liz's second bragging right was that she designed costumes for several of the high school plays. Her favorite design experience was for the play "Camelot" because she got to work with Sister Barnard. Sister Barnard was the seamstress of Liz's creations. "It was a memorable experience to serve in a kind of professional capacity alongside my teacher and mentor," Liz recalls. Sister Barnard was recognized in the community for her exceptional sewing skills. Although she enjoyed sewing as a hobby, Sister Barnard had the skill set to be a professional.

Third, and perhaps the most interesting, was Liz's boyfriends—or rather her romantic interests. Liz had her first date with Marty Reeder. They met on the school bus in junior high and went to a boy-girl party at a friend's house. "He was the nicest boy," Liz recalls. They remain friends to this day. Then there was Dan Price—though there was never a date with Dan, a budding young actor in the high school productions—there was a lot of flirting going on at play practices. Bruce Garrett, a nephew of her seminary teacher Dean Garrett, was her date to the Sadie Hawkins dance. In each case, Liz asked the young men to the dates, which never sat well with her father.

As with most teenagers, Liz reflects back on her high school years and wonders why so many of her friends see them as "the glory years." She had bragging rights with the Rockettes and costumes created for school plays, but she sees such recognition as fleeting, nothing more. Wanting to date and not being asked had a more lasting impact, as did never being embraced by the social elite in high school. Life ahead proved much more interesting

Life after High School

The summer after high school graduation in 1971, Liz met Rod Lemon—a handsome, popular young man who looked like Matt Damon.

Rod was older than Liz and had attended a year of college at Weber State. When Rod asked Liz on a date, it was a real date and she was swept off her feet. She was impressed because he asked and was interested in her. It was a whirlwind summer of romance, fast cars, parties at Willard Bay, and fun. But there was an issue—Rod was known in Willard, the adjoining town south of Perry, as a "borderline bad boy." Although he was old enough to serve a mission, he never considered serving the Lord. There were other issues too.

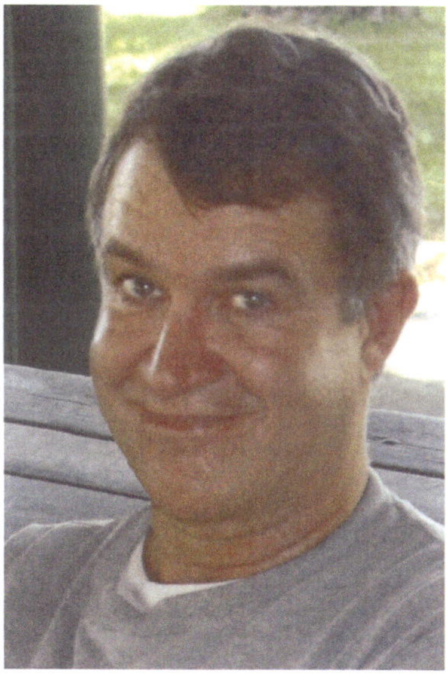

When autumn came, most of the college-bound teenagers in Perry and Willard lived at home and commuted to Weber State. Liz's father saw red flags in his daughter's romantic relationship with Rod, and in an effort to curtail it, he paid for Liz to live in Stansbury Hall, a residence hall on the Weber State campus. It didn't help. When not attending college classes, Liz found every reason to be with Rod. Romance blossomed and Liz fell madly in love.

In June 1972, Liz married Rod Lemon. One of the red flags her father saw was her slipping further and further away from the Church. By the time of her marriage, neither Rod nor Liz was active. In fact, Liz took every possible Sunday shift at Maddox Ranch House to avoid the guilt she was feeling. Her father encouraged Liz and Rod to get back into activity in the Church so they could be sealed in the Ogden Temple. At first they both rejected the idea, but over the next few months they began to soften.

With reality comes perspective, or maybe with perspective comes reality. Either way Liz recognized that the love she thought she had for Rod wasn't love at all. "Rod stood for everything that had been denied me—he was popular and his family had money and he had always wanted to become a surgeon," Liz says. "He was the first boy that ever looked at me twice. I didn't think that I was good enough for anyone else. I let my guard down." When Liz reflects on that time in her life, she always comes away with the idea that "one of the most important gifts a parent can give a child is self-esteem. It is such a critical factor in every decision the child will make. To truly live life to the fullest—self-esteem must play a major role. It's not enough to point out all the things the child is good at or all the potential the child possesses; parents must teach their children the value of their spirits, their divine birthright."

The next nineteen years in Liz's life brought pain, sorrow, five children, career changes, and nineteen moves in as many years. Rod changed his mind about becoming a surgeon. He decided instead to work for the United States Department of the Interior. With his new goal firm, Rod concluded that he and Liz should attend Utah State University, an agricultural land grant university nestled in the hills of Logan. Liz could see little advantage for her to make such a move. She was taking classes in art and fashion design and liked her professors at Weber State. A visiting professor from Harvard was teaching her art history and theory. "If I didn't have the skill to draw, I would have loved to teach art history like he did," Liz says. Then there was

Professor Groberg who taught anatomy and Professor Collette who taught illustration. Liz was pursuing a degree in Fashion Illustration and Design, one of her many dreams. A university that took pride in agriculture like Utah State in Logan was not the right choice for her, but in her pursuit of fashion design, neither was Weber State. After all, Utah was where fashion came to die.

Against Liz's wishes, she and Rod moved to Logan. Rod completed his bachelor's degree in wildlife management and range science and a master's program in natural resources and chemistry. Through his years of schooling Liz was expected to be a young mother and the breadwinner of the family. She painted portraits for thirty dollars apiece and worked part-time at The Real McCoy Art Gallery on Main Street in Logan. Of necessity, her schooling almost came to a standstill. The only time she could attend classes was when a neighbor was willing to trade babysitting responsibilities.

Nevertheless, Liz threw herself into the arts. Professor Marion Hyde, once her high school teacher and now Dean of the Art Department at Utah State, encouraged Liz to find her passion in art. In that process Liz discovered that she had a passion for drawing and painting the human form. While most budding artists shy away from painting faces and hands, she rallied to the challenge. "It came to me as naturally as if it were a calling," Liz says.

Moving to Provo

Liz and Rod would have continued their educational pursuits at Utah State had not an art professor told Liz, "A scout from Osmond Studios in Provo is here looking for artists to work on the Donny and Marie Show. Are you interested?" Liz was not only interested but excited about the possible opportunity. The mere thought of working for a major studio sounded glamorous and impressive. She envisioned herself being a designer for the Osmonds as a way to move her career forward and a chance to solve mounting financial problems. She convinced Rod that he should pursue his master's degree at Brigham Young University while she worked at the studio. Rod liked the idea.

Soon Liz was driving to Provo to meet with Bill Bohnert, a representative from Los Angeles for the Osmonds. Bohnert hired Liz on the spot.

Within six weeks Liz and Rod had moved their family of now four children to Provo so Liz could work full-time for the Osmonds and Rod could pursue a master's degree in range science. For two years Liz was one of six designers mixing paints and working on sets in what was sarcastically called "the kitchen" of the studio. She had the distinction of being the only female painter, which meant that she received less money for doing the same work as her male counterparts and had no possibility of promotion. Then there was the issue of choosing the set designer.

In her interview with Bohnert, Liz understood that her job would be designing sets for the Donny and Marie variety show. The painful reality was she now painted the designs of others. She was a set painter, the least glamorous job in the studio. Liz would be handed a design and script on Monday for a film-taping that would take place on Saturday. Her job was to get the sets painted and ready. Some days this meant arriving at the studio as early as six a.m. and not returning home until after midnight. Liz worked long hours on frantic projects and then had a hiatus that could last as long as three months. When left with no work and told to wait for the next series to be filmed, there was no income.

Wanting to solve the problem of employee downtime and advance the recognition of the Osmond Studios, shows from Los Angeles and New York were brought to the Provo studio. The new shows had a worldly element that wasn't conducive to the gospel standards practiced by most studio employees. Liz was ready to move away from the studio but Rod was only halfway through his masters' program and contributed nothing to the family income. Liz needed the money that the studio provided; yet she knew it was time to quit when her favorite activity at work was pulling cable for the cameraman on film day. "What I really wanted to do was paint," Liz says.

Meanwhile Rod successfully matriculated through his master's degree and his thesis, "The Migration of Flight Patterns of the Cedar-wax Wing," a subject that held little interest for Liz. Rod planned his schedule so that he could be home with the children while Liz was at work, but she didn't like the arrangement. Coming home late at night, Liz felt guilty that she hadn't been with her children and when she was at home Rod was off looking for birds in the sky and becoming a crippling perfectionist to himself and his family. Liz couldn't understand why Rod struggled so hard to meet deadlines and why every word spoken in his presence had to be pronounced phonetically correct. His impatience with everyone, especially his family, and his inability to interact in social settings were just a few of the difficulties Liz dealt with. Then there was the simple fact that Liz was always exhausted. Years later Rod was diagnosed with Asperger's syndrome, but at the time, Liz couldn't understand Rod's reasoning, and it was a burden to her and her young family.

A Struggling Artist

When Osmond Studios finally closed their doors, other television shows were brought into the building. There was now a seedy side to her work and Liz quit. She was happy to be home with her children but the financial hardship of living on savings took its toll on the family. Wanting to alleviate the ever-present financial stress, Liz took a few of her art pieces to show furniture store dealers and interior decorators in Salt Lake City. She hoped they would like her work and want to promote it. She even flew to Washington, D.C. to meet with personnel of May Company to sell prints in their furniture departments nationwide. What the designers and furniture executives wanted was paintings of ducks with an Americana motif. At the time, gingham and calico ducks were the rage. It was not unusual to see fabric collages of ducks and stuffed ducks placed on fireplace hearths and on over-stuffed granny sofas, even in high-end homes.

To paint Americana art is a real craft and Liz didn't have the skill. But believing such paintings were her ticket to financial freedom, she devoured books on the anatomy of ducks. She wanted to be anatomically correct and to go beyond the Americana approach to something more sophisticated. Liz didn't want her ducks to be just one- or two-dimensional; they had to be

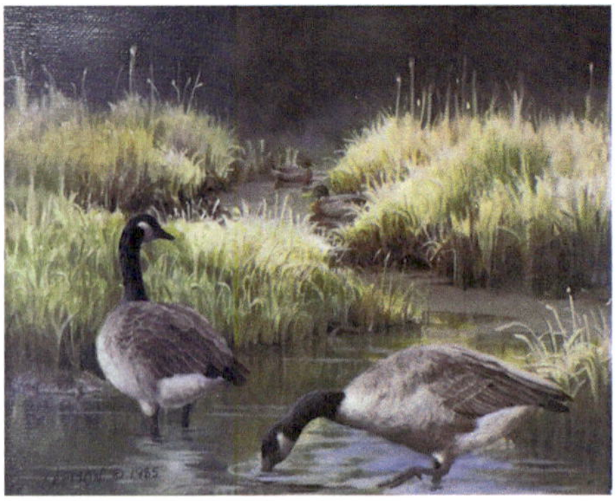

unique. In creating her own style, Liz overshot the market and disappointed interior decorators and furniture executives alike. Liz says, "I was a dismal failure and really miserable. I still had my family to support and didn't know how to advance my career."

The answer to her queries came when Liz saw the art of Nancy Glazier in an article titled "Beauty and the Beast" in the *Southwest Art Magazine.* Liz literally lost her breath looking at Nancy's paintings of buffaloes. Liz wanted to learn her technique. Although Liz lived just ten miles from Nancy, it took her days to muster up the courage to telephone. When she finally did, Liz explained her background in art and asked if Nancy would tutor her. Liz told Nancy that she had no money, but she could clean her house, prepare her meals, and tend her children in exchange for lessons. Nancy briskly replied, "I have no time for that, maybe you could call so and so and see if they do that kind of thing."

As the days and weeks passed, Liz prayed that Nancy Glazier would reconsider and hear her out before hanging up the phone. She prayed that Nancy's heart would soften and that the Spirit would somehow speak to her. When Liz finally got the courage to call Nancy back, she braced for the worst. She was surprised when Nancy answered the telephone and said, "I'm so glad you called." "Nancy couldn't remembered my name but the Spirit had been working on her," Liz says. "She didn't know how to reach me and felt bad about how she had responded to my request. She invited me to come to her home and bring my portfolio. She promised to look at my art and offer suggestions.

"With a portfolio filled with the best samples of my work, I entered the home of Nancy Glazier," Liz says. "Nancy invited me to place my sketches around the edges of her living room and dining room floors. Nancy then looked at my artwork. There was silence until Nancy said, 'These aren't very good! You've got a lot of work to do. It'll take you fifteen years before your career breaks. You have to live long enough and experience enough life to be good—really good. I'll show you how to succeed.' I was angry and replied, 'I don't have fifteen years—I will do it in one.' Nancy said, 'It's not negotiable.'"

Liz thought, *I'll show you.* But through the passing years, Liz came to realize that Nancy was right almost to the day about her career. She did need to live life, refine life, and filter her work through life's ups and downs. She had to master her skill with at least ten thousand hours of practice. Such a prospect was daunting, and Liz had to ask herself whether she was ready to commit that much time to her talent or drop out of art and get a regular job. That day Liz made the decision to start over in her art career under the guidance of one of the best, if not the best, wildlife artists in the world.

For two years Liz went to Nancy's home nearly every day, sometimes having to enter through the back door past the live buffaloes. Sitting next to Nancy at her easel, Liz watched her paint and listened to her every word. Liz was blessed to be "taught at the feet of the master" and she knew it. Every day she thanked her Heavenly Father for this once-in-a-lifetime opportunity. Nancy didn't just teach the technical aspects of her craft—she taught her passion. When Liz became discouraged, Nancy was right there with words of encouragement.

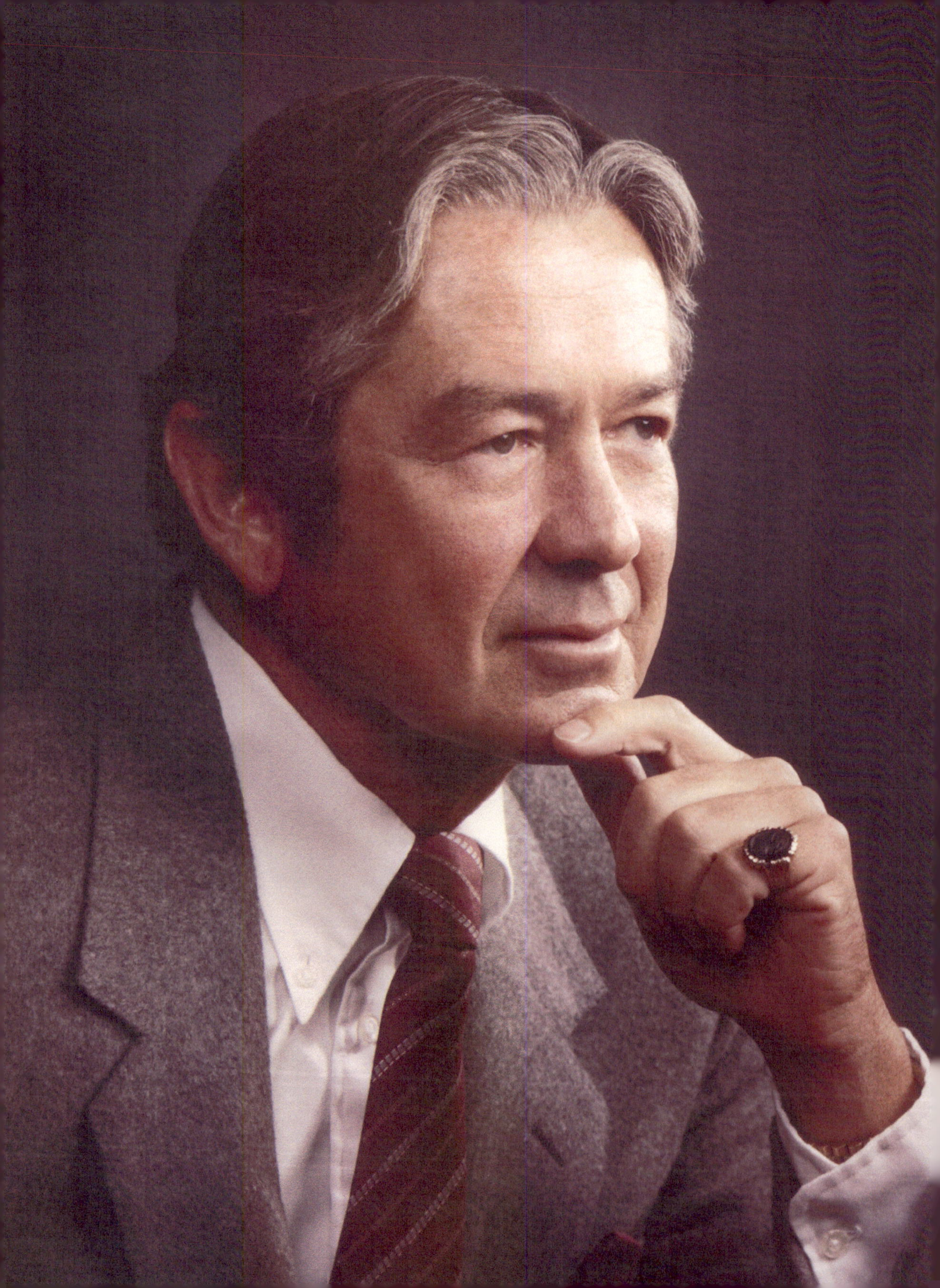

The Beginnings of Success

Liz's first big break came when Nancy invited her to attend a convention of the Wild Wings franchises held in Lake City, Minnesota. Nancy was confident that Liz would meet buyers at the convention who would purchase her waterfowl paintings. She suggested that a representative from a Wild Wing franchise might even select Liz's work for his gallery. As Liz was pulling prints for Nancy to sign at the convention, she met David Maass, a world-renowned waterfowl artist and lead artist for Wild Wings. More importantly, she met Arthur Bond (pictured left), who talked of his Wild Wings franchise and gallery in Santa Rosa, California. Just as Nancy had predicted, Bond asked Liz if he could display her art in his gallery.

Within weeks, Bond sold Liz's first waterfowl painting for 1,200 dollars and sent her a check for 732 dollars. Liz was thrilled beyond words. For years she had painted in the corner of her unfinished basement, but with newfound success she stuffed her children in two of three bedrooms and turned the third one into an art studio. (Liz's daughter Loree remembers helping her paint grass at age five.)

Although Bond had only one gallery at the time, checks arrived every month. When the art market was slow Bond advanced Liz money, confident that her paintings would sell. He was also proactive in introducing Liz's work to collectors and in creating a strong collector's base. As Bond was building Liz's art reputation, like gallery owners are supposed to do, he made Liz aware of the Pacific Flyway Decoy Auction and Show being held in Sacramento, California. At this popular trade show buyers purchased duck whistles, guns, waterfowl art, and brass faucets with handles shaped like ducks. At the show Liz met Paul Prudler, a venture capitalist and avid hunter with a passion for waterfowl paintings. Prudler purchased three of Liz's original paintings and later flew her to the Sutter Buttes Mountain Range so she could photograph his favorite place to hunt and paint the range into one of the paintings he had purchased.

Liz became an acclaimed artist among duck hunters and customers at several Wild Wing franchises. Soon her art was picked up by the May Galleries in Jackson Hole, Wyoming, and Scottsdale, Arizona, and by another gallery in Honolulu, Hawaii. Liz welcomed the recognition and was willing to listen as gallery owners encouraged her to paint more than ducks—big game like elk and moose. "There's a market in game animals for you," they said. To their customers they said, "Liz Lemon is another Nancy Glazier." But that wasn't exactly the case. Liz's paintings sold for 7,000 to 8,000 dollars whereas Nancy's sold in the 60,000 dollar range. Yet Liz did sell a painting of a buffalo to an insurance company for 10,800 dollars. More impressive than the high price tag was when Liz placed in the top one hundred artists in the Federal Duck Stamp Contest. She was flown to Ocean City, Maryland, where her paintings were displayed with other finalists.

Liz's paintings of wildlife were now in great demand. She would often ship a painting wet to an anxious buyer. Sometimes answering a phone call would result in a commission for a painting that needed to be started and shipped in four days to a gallery. The stress on Liz was real but so was her talent. Collectors and gallery owners saw Liz as the alternative for buyers who couldn't afford the works of Nancy Glazier. They were more than willing to sell works that were nearly as good as the famous wildlife artist without the expensive price tag.

When Nancy Glazier moved to a ranch in Montana, Liz began working with Nancy's framer, Art Phesey. Phesey showed one of Liz's paintings to Russell Parks, the owner of Parks Sporting in Orem. Phesey had hoped that Parks would purchase the painting and said, "Liz Lemon paints just like Nancy Glazier but her cost is more reasonable." Parks saw Liz's work as a threat to Nancy and brought it to the attention of the renowned artist.

Although copying can be the greatest form of flattery, when the student begins to improve, it can make the teacher nervous. Nancy had grown nervous so she went to Orem to speak with Liz about her paintings. She reproved Liz, claiming Liz's work was bordering plagiarism and said, "I don't want you to paint Yellowstone." Nancy felt Liz was encroaching on her artistic territory.

The irony of the confrontation was that Liz had grown weary of painting fur, landscapes, and wilderness habitats. She was no longer interested in painting big game. But Nancy was right—collectors were buying Liz's work instead of hers because of cost and that was infringing on Nancy's market.

Although Liz knew Nancy had a right to be upset, and wanted to appease her, she was conflicted. If she backed away from painting buffaloes and other large game animals, the prestigious May Galleries would drop her. Liz approached Dan May, owner of the May Galleries and presented her dilemma to him. He agreed that Nancy's rights were being stepped on, but he also knew that Liz had broken no laws and she was making him money. Liz stewed for days over her impending decision to stop painting wild animals or face another confrontation with Nancy.

Shifting Focus

During this conflicted time, Dan May telephoned Liz with a request to submit a painting to the Arts for Parks competition. It was the first year of the competition and the purse was 100,000 dollars. The guidelines of the competition were simple: paint one of the national parks, enter it in the competition, and hope to win. The problem with Dan's request was landscapes were not Liz's strength and she had lost her desire to paint big game. Dan was insistent that she consider entering the contest. Liz hung up the phone feeling very agitated.

In the days that followed, Liz mulled over several ideas she could paint for the Arts for Parks competition, none of which were very interesting. Then one day as she was taking the trash out, she stepped into the carport, looked up, and saw her reflection in the car window. It was then she got the idea to paint what it was like to vacation at a national park.

From her childhood, Liz could only think of a handful of times her family went on a vacation. Every time, it was hot and she and her siblings sat in the back seat of the car and argued and whined with relentless hunger pains. Liz remembered one such vacation to Zion's National Park to see the Great White Throne, a mountain structure that looked nothing like a throne. It took hours to get to Zion. She recalls no air-conditioning in the car and her father whistling most of the way, unaware of the mutiny going on in the back seat because he was deaf. Upon entering the park, it was only a few minutes before Liz and her family saw the Great White Throne. "We got out of the car, Dad pointed out the object of the trip, and we got back in the car, begging all the while for a bathroom," Liz recalls. "With potty detail out of the way we headed home, arriving several hours later, exhausted, grumpy, and argumentative. Soda

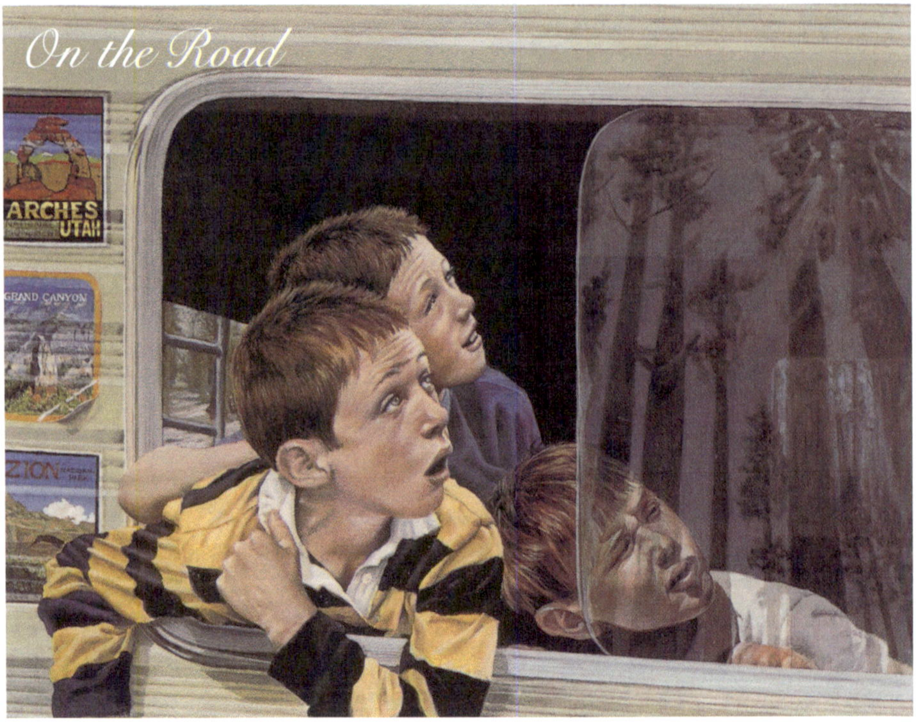

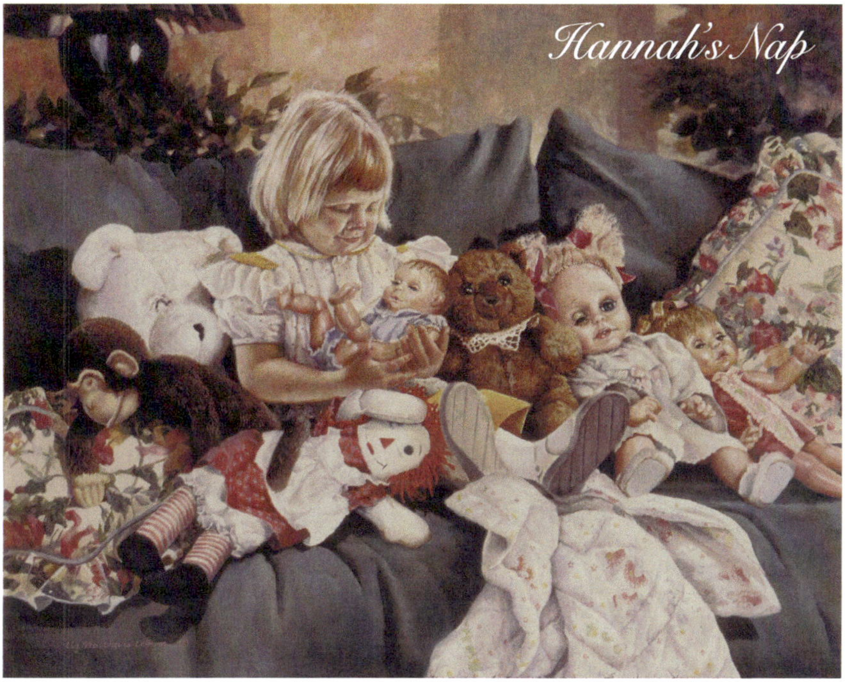

crackers were smashed into the car seat where we once sat. That was our family trip to a national park."

Liz painted the park as an "in-your-face piece." To her surprise she won the Founder's Favorite Award, fifth in the competition out of 2,700-plus entries. Liz shared the award with Thomas Kinkade, much to his dislike of having to share an award with a "nobody." As James Watts, US Secretary of the Interior, handed Liz the award, she didn't feel like a "nobody." Liz knew that she had succeeded. More importantly, she knew that she could paint children in comical situation or in real-life situations and her paintings would sell—the mayor of Jackson Hole, Wyoming, purchased "On the Road" within a week, and Kraft Foods executives expressed interested in using the painting in a promotional campaign as a launch into a commercial. Although nothing came of the latter, Liz was confident painting artworks of children was the right career move. Dan May agreed and promised to carry "On the Road" in his Scottsdale and Jackson Hole galleries. Liz next sent "Hannah's Nap" to Dan; he sold it in his Orem gallery. Like "On the Road," "Hannah's Nap" sold quickly.

Struggles at Home

On the surface, Liz's world was easing as gallery owners spoke of the versatility of her art and clamored with each other for her originals. Yet at home Liz's world was becoming more difficult. The difficulty stemmed from what Liz called the "organized turmoil" of her marriage to Rod. He had finished his degree at Brigham Young University and accepted employment as a chemist with Geneva Steel. When the steel plant closed its doors, Rod worked for Parrish Chemicals located near the defunct steel plant. Although he tried to be the breadwinner of the family, it wasn't working. "His paycheck couldn't support our family of five children," Liz recalls. Adding to the issue Rod was disgruntled and ill-tempered about not being employed by the US Department of Interior and blamed President Ronald Reagan for imposing a "freeze" on hiring new government employees.

Liz often asked herself, "Can I stay in the marriage for the sake of the children?" She muses, "I married Rod because he asked me out when others didn't. He was from a prominent family and my family wasn't prominent in anything. Rod had a promising future as a surgeon and then as a government employee, but ended up stuck in a chemical job that couldn't pay the bills."

Rod became more neglectful, shortsighted, and ill-tempered with each passing day. An impasse was reached the day their daughter Mishel failed to close the door after letting the dog outside. Rod, who was seated within an arm's length of the door, told Mishel to shut it. "I'm in a hurry," Mishel replied. Rod screamed out a tirade of profanity and insisted that she come at once and shut the door. As Mishel turned to Liz, Liz saw a pleading in her daughter's eyes that clearly said, "Mom, help me." Liz knew that Rod was not physically abusive to the children, but his caustic words were destroying their confidence. Liz knew if she stayed in the marriage any longer, Mishel, Loree, and Jenifer would marry men just like Rod. Liz couldn't bear to see them go through what she had for the past nineteen years.

Liz knew at that moment it was time to end the marriage. "You can destroy a child with words," Liz says. "I decided to do something about the escalating problem. Mistakes can direct our lives only as long as we let them. It was time for my children and me to take a different path. My decision was to raise the children alone. The best thing that came from my marriage was my five children—Steevun, Bryun, Mishel, Loree, and Jenifer."

In the divorce proceedings Liz didn't ask for alimony or child support. "Rod was left in an awful place and I knew he was as unhappy as I was," Liz says. "I didn't want to cripple him with a financial burden when he needed money to get on his feet." The judge ordered Rod to pay a monthly fee of fifty dollars per child. In September 1991, Liz signed the divorce papers.

To his credit, Rod promised to stay out of the picture for a while so the children could bond with a new father. Liz thought this odd, for although she wanted to marry and find happiness in marriage, she never thought it would be possible. After all, she was thirty-nine years old with five children in the home.

New Horizons

As Liz moved on with her life, there was much inner turmoil that was slow to subside. She regretted betraying a promise to her father to be kind to Rod. She was weighed down with the realization that she had failed at the most basic thing in life—marriage. She felt humiliated as former friends gossiped and pointed an accusing finger at her. Her bishop, mindful of their hurtful words, took Liz out of the line of fire by calling her to serve in the ward library along with Katie Harris and Barbara Louder, sisters.

As it turned out, Katie and Barbara were just what Liz needed. They made her laugh when nothing in her life was funny. Every Sunday they would give her a pep talk. They would jokingly tell Liz to pull up her bra straps, put on some lipstick, and not look back. They laughed with her and cried with her, and slowly Liz began to heal. "Stand up straight and find a man," Katie said. "We talked like chattering hens each Sunday," Liz recalls. "They let me wonder aloud if I would ever remarry. They helped me gain perspective on life, be hopeful about my future, and like myself again. These two wonderful friends saved me."

At the encouragement of her library friends, Liz attended LDS dances for older adults—with mixed results. When she refused to dance with a ninety-five-year-old man, he yelled in the church foyer, "You think you're too good for me!" Although Liz kept one foot in the single scene and navigated her way through a maze of "undesirables," her main focus was on being a mother and a breadwinner. Her children thrived and excelled in school and with friends. She had every reason to be proud of them. She wanted them to be proud of her too.

About this time Liz saw a need to improve her figure drawing skills in order to take her paintings to the next level. She enrolled in a class at the Springville Art Museum arranged by Gary Price, a Wild Wings artist like herself. "Short of digging up a cadaver, the only way I was ever going to understand the human form was to attend a figure drawing class with nude models, and that was what the museum offered," Liz says. "Wearing a leotard hides too much of the muscle definition." But one day as she put her hand on the doorknob and attempted to enter the class, Liz felt prompted to leave immediately. She got back in her car and drove home, not understanding why. That night a local news channel aired the story of concerned citizens protesting the art class, claiming "the class smacked of pornography." Television reporters interviewed several artists who were in class that day.

"I felt protected on that occasion and never went back to class," Liz says. "I had never been opposed to anatomy classes. Classical realism requires a good understanding of the human body. Neither Weber State nor Utah State offered such classes and as far as I knew, Utah Valley College didn't either. I knew that BYU would likely not offer such a course so it was understandable that a class like this was formed in the private art community. Most professional artists in the area have passed through that class at one time or another, but that day it was imperative that I didn't attend. I came to realize that if I had been one of the artists interviewed that day it would likely have had a negative effect on the later success of my Joseph Smith project. Most people don't understand the need for such a class. That is why a class like the one offered at the Springville Art Museum always comes under fire.

"Without the class and knowing that I needed instruction," Liz says, "I asked my Heavenly Father to help me see and understand the human form well enough to paint the paintings I would one day be commissioned to paint. The Lord blessed me immediately in ways that I've never been able to explain."

Expanding Horizons

"There's good and bad about staying home painting every day," Liz says. "I sent paintings to the galleries on a regular basis and met deadlines, but I missed interacting with adults." It was Sharon Swindle, owner of Frameworks at the University Mall in Orem, who suggested that Liz work a few hours each week for her company. Sharon thought a few hours in her Orem store would give Liz a chance to be with adults and learn the business side of art. Liz was flattered by the offer since Frameworks was the gallery of choice in Utah County. The Swindles also operated stores in Salt Lake, Foothill, and West Valley.

Liz enjoyed interacting with customers who frequented Frameworks, but what she really wanted was a chance to show Sharon Swindle her artwork. Sharon, a pioneer of art in Utah, had an unusual talent for recognizing exceptional local artists. When Liz finally showed Sharon her best paintings, Sharon embraced Liz and convinced her that Frameworks should be her gallery.

As Liz frequented Frameworks more often to display her paintings, she noticed Sharon's son Bucky in the back room. He was a shy and introverted bachelor, barely looking up from his computer to acknowledge the presence of anyone, let alone Liz. "Bucky was stand-offish," Liz recalls. "He didn't comb his hair or tie his shoes. His shirts were wrinkled. He didn't catch my attention as a dating prospect—he didn't fit the mold. I pictured dating a man in a suit who wore loafers and carried a briefcase." Yet Liz delighted in startling Bucky with her off-the-wall comments like, "When are you taking me to Vegas?" Bucky would look up from his computer and acknowledge her question, yet remain aloof.

There wasn't any mutual interest between the two until the day Liz's paintings were featured in a Christmas show at the Foothill Repartee Gallery in Salt Lake. As Liz drove to the gallery she hoped Bucky would be there, but entertaining such a thought made her feel vulnerable, conspicuous, and awkward. As fate would have it Bucky did come to the Christmas show but stayed in the back room and worked on the computer. He never came out to talk to customers or to Liz. Taking the initiative, Liz went to the back room and goaded Bucky into talking to her. In so doing Liz discovered an interest in what he had to say. Bucky listened intently to her opinions and expressed tender responses—qualities Liz hadn't seen in any man except her father. She left the show thinking Bucky had an infectious dry wit, was very funny, scary smart, and unusually kind.

Following that Christmas encounter Liz and Bucky found reasons to be together at other gallery events. Liz looked forward to their conversations and listening to Bucky's perception on myriad topics. It felt good to talk to a man who listened and understood. Sometimes Liz and Bucky would laugh until they felt silly, other times they were serious. One night, after Bucky had driven Liz home and parked his car in the driveway, Liz sat in his car and talked for two hours. During those hours her children kept poking their heads out of the drapes wondering when their mother would come inside. When her painting "Heroes: Like Nephi of Old" was printed in the *Friend* magazine, the first person Liz wanted to tell was Bucky—even though she was dating someone else at the time. She drove to the Frameworks warehouse in East Bay to show him the magazine. He was genuinely excited for Liz and ended up talking with her until two in the morning.

It was not long before Bucky had endeared himself to not only Liz, but her children as well. When Jenifer answered the door dressed as Miss Scarlet in the "Game of Clue," Bucky ran back to his car and picked up a beret he had purchased in Italy. He came back to the door and introduced himself as Professor Plum. The children laughed. Bucky brought Steevun home late one evening from an Arnold Friberg art show while Steevun was working for Frameworks. As was characteristic of Liz's children, Steevun stood in Liz's bedroom doorway to report to her on his evening. Being 6'6", Steevun gripped the top of the doorframe and asked, "What do you think of Bucky?"

"He did not wait for my answer," Liz says. Steevun blurted out, "I think you should marry him."

Not long after that incident, Bucky was driving Liz home and asked, "When are you going to ask me to marry you?" Liz was startled and uneasy

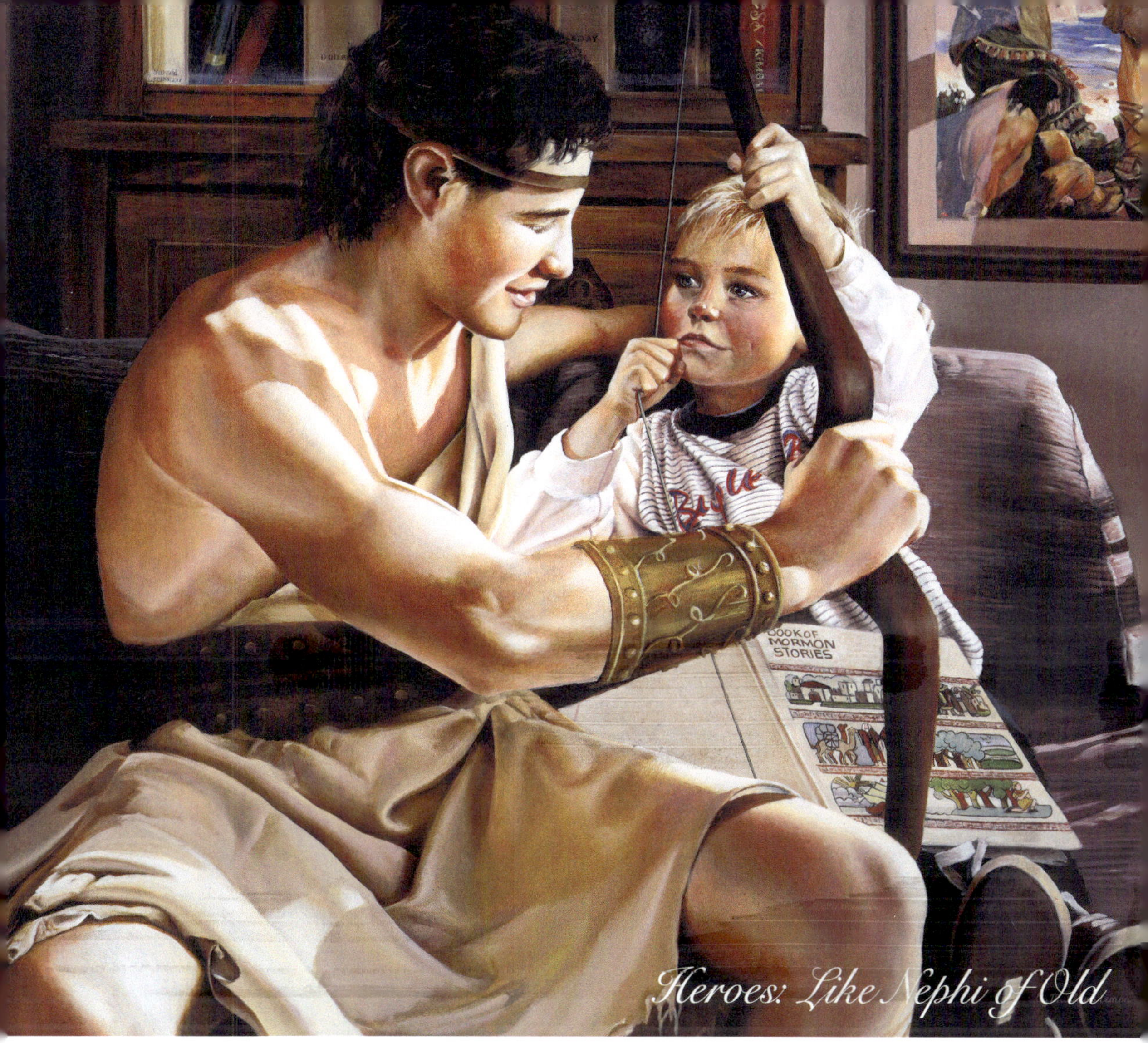

with his joking about such a serious matter. She asked him to stop the car and pull over. She asked why he was making such comments and asked him to take her home, which he did. Later that night Bucky telephoned Liz and said, "I just wanted you to know that I am serious." Despite the fact that Bucky was moving way too fast in their relationship, Liz couldn't dismiss him or his unorthodox proposal.

At the same time Liz was seeing Bucky, she was casually seeing another man. She wasn't serious about either one of them, but the question she couldn't dismiss was, "Why not marry Bucky?" As she did with most of her decisions,

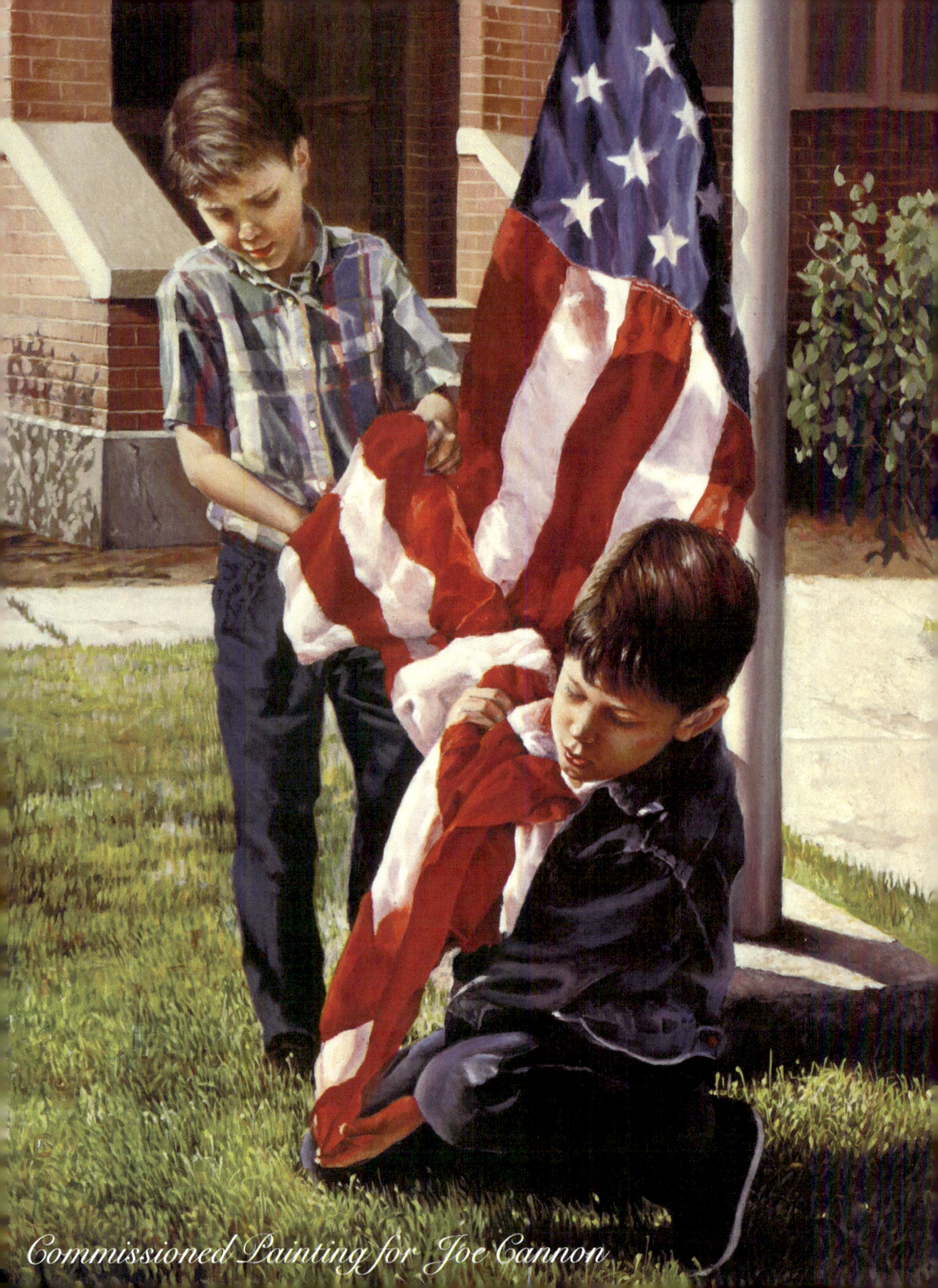

Commissioned Painting for Joe Cannon

Liz made a list of pros and cons comparing Bucky to the other man. The column under Bucky's name was easily filled compared to the three things she liked about the other man. Liz thought to herself how silly this was, but the feeling wouldn't leave her. Liz slipped to her knees and asked with a pleading heart, "What should I do? I can't fail at marriage again. I hardly know either of these men, but I like so many things about Bucky." As Liz rose to her feet, she had the overwhelming impression that Bucky would help her return to her Heavenly Father. That was enough for her.

Moving Forward in Faith

Liz telephoned Bucky to tell him to meet her the next day. She was going to be at a school in Provo doing a photo shoot with Joe Cannon's sons and she asked Bucky to meet her there. After the photo shoot Liz and Bucky drove up Spanish Fork Canyon, and at her suggestion Bucky pulled off the side of the road and they stepped out of the car. It was early March—the weather was sunny and cold. Shivering, Liz told Bucky that she would marry him. Before she could say another word, Bucky grabbed her and swung her around with such excitement that she was reminded of a merry-go-round. As strange as it all felt, Liz was delighted. Up to this point, Bucky had been quiet and reserved. To see this side of him was almost delightful. Liz remarks, "If any of my daughters ever came home and told me they wanted to marry the man they had only known for a few weeks, I would have shipped them off to some undisclosed location where they would never be found again." Yet marrying Bucky felt right. Liz was at peace.

But as time went by and she and Bucky set the marriage date Liz began to worry. She had been obsessed with the importance of the outward appearance her entire life. She was about to marry a man that didn't see the necessity of tying his shoes nor any particular reason to comb his hair. He fit the mold of an absent-minded professor. Liz knew these things shouldn't matter yet they were getting in the way every time she saw Bucky. Out of frustration Liz went to the Lord asking for help. She presented the Lord with a list of all the things that irritated her about Bucky until she simply stopped and asked, "Please let me see him through your eyes." Before Liz could get back on her feet, her fears were gone. She saw a Christlike man who would always love the Lord first and her second. Liz could trust his priorities because she knew Bucky would cherish his new family. She has never gone back to that place where such silly things matter, but she still doesn't let Bucky out the door without first taking a comb to his hair. The shoes get tied without her help.

Telling Bucky's family of their impending nuptials was a lot of fun. To say everyone in his family was delighted is an understatement. Her friends were a different matter, however. They initially thought Liz was joking about marrying Bucky but saw within seconds that she was serious—some voiced concerns and others were just dumbfounded. In the end, all were concerned her marriage was too soon. Liz's divorce was final on September 9, 1991, and she was planning to remarry eight months later. Even Liz agreed that it was too fast, but she assured friends that her decision was right and her children were elated. They loved Bucky from the night he came in the door as Professor Plum.

Bucky and Liz went to see Bishop Williams about applying for a temple cancellation of Liz's temple sealing to Rod. They were told it would take at least a year and likely longer before a cancellation could be granted. "We were disappointed," Liz says. "We decided to marry in the temple for time." The Sunday before the marriage ceremony Liz filed for a cancellation and hoped for the best. About six o'clock the night before her wedding on May 9, 1992, Liz received a telephone call from Bishop Williams. The bishop asked her how much she loved Bucky and how long she wanted to be married to him. Both were very strange questions, but perfectly reasonable coming from him. Liz replied, "I love Bucky very much and hope to one day be sealed to him for eternity." The bishop could hardly hold back. "You got your wish," he said with excitement. "Your cancellation was granted. You are free to be sealed to him for eternity tomorrow in the ceremony." Needless to say, Liz called Bucky immediately and they cried on the phone together.

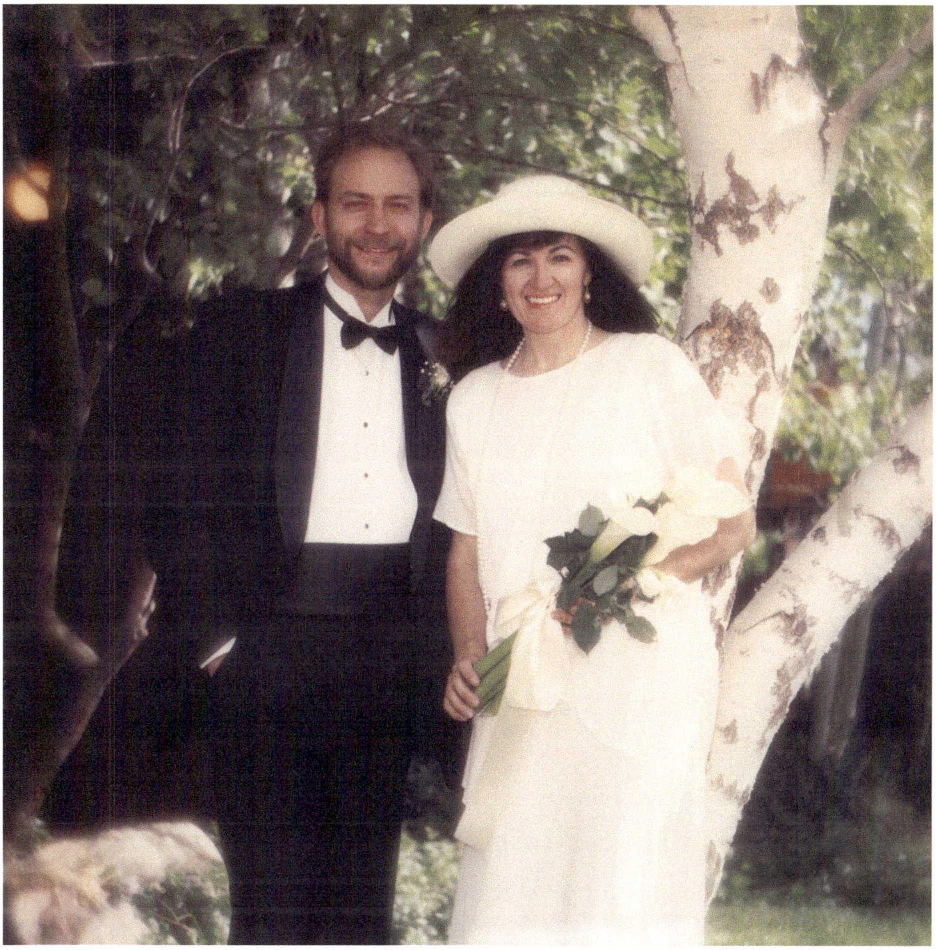

Financial Freedom or Personal Fulfillment?

On the honeymoon, Liz asked Bucky about his job at Frameworks. She never thought to ask before because she had always been responsible for the financial well-being of her family. She just figured it would continue that way. Bucky laughed and said, "I own it." Years previously, he and his parents bought the company and had been running it ever since—about twenty years to be precise.

When the newlyweds returned home from their honeymoon, Bucky handed Liz an envelope and told her to open it. Inside was a gold American Express card. Liz looked a little puzzled and asked, "What am I supposed to do with this?"

"Go shopping," Bucky replied. "Look at the name on the card—it's your name, Liz Swindle. I want you to go out and spend some money. That's my wedding gift to you. You never have to paint again unless you want to." Liz was overcome.

The next two years Liz shopped and shopped. Shoes, dresses, more shoes, dishes, pans, more shoes, gadgets, and doohickeys—there was no end to her wants. Shopping bags galore sat in her closet unopened for months with the tags still on the purchased items. Liz felt empty. In contrast, Bucky came home from Frameworks excited to share stories of the success of artists Greg Olsen and James C. Christensen. Liz found herself becoming pretty jealous hearing about all their successes in the art world and realizing that's what was missing in her life. She had been out of the business for two years and would have to start over if she wanted to jump back in. Liz thought she could re-enter the market painting children, but her youngest daughter Jenifer was turning eleven years old and her interest in painting young children had waned.

One day Liz saw a young boy wearing a Superman cape walking with his father down the street. She overheard the father and son talk about how the little boy could fly like Superman. She was very taken with the scene and had a brother-in-law and his son reenact the scene while being photographed. Within days her painting, "Even Superman Needs a Dad," was on canvas.

Almost overnight the iconic painting became a huge success. The emotional high that Liz hadn't found in shopping sprees was back. She was ready to jump in the middle of the art market in a big way but unsure of the first step.

For a time Liz thought the four-year-old neighbor boy Ross held the key. In the morning his mass of blonde hair looked as if his mother had ratted it with a comb. When Liz asked the boy about his hair, he said with a straight face, "The hair fairies attack my hair while I'm sleeping." His words resonated with Liz and she painted "Hair Fairies."

Even Superman Needs a Dad

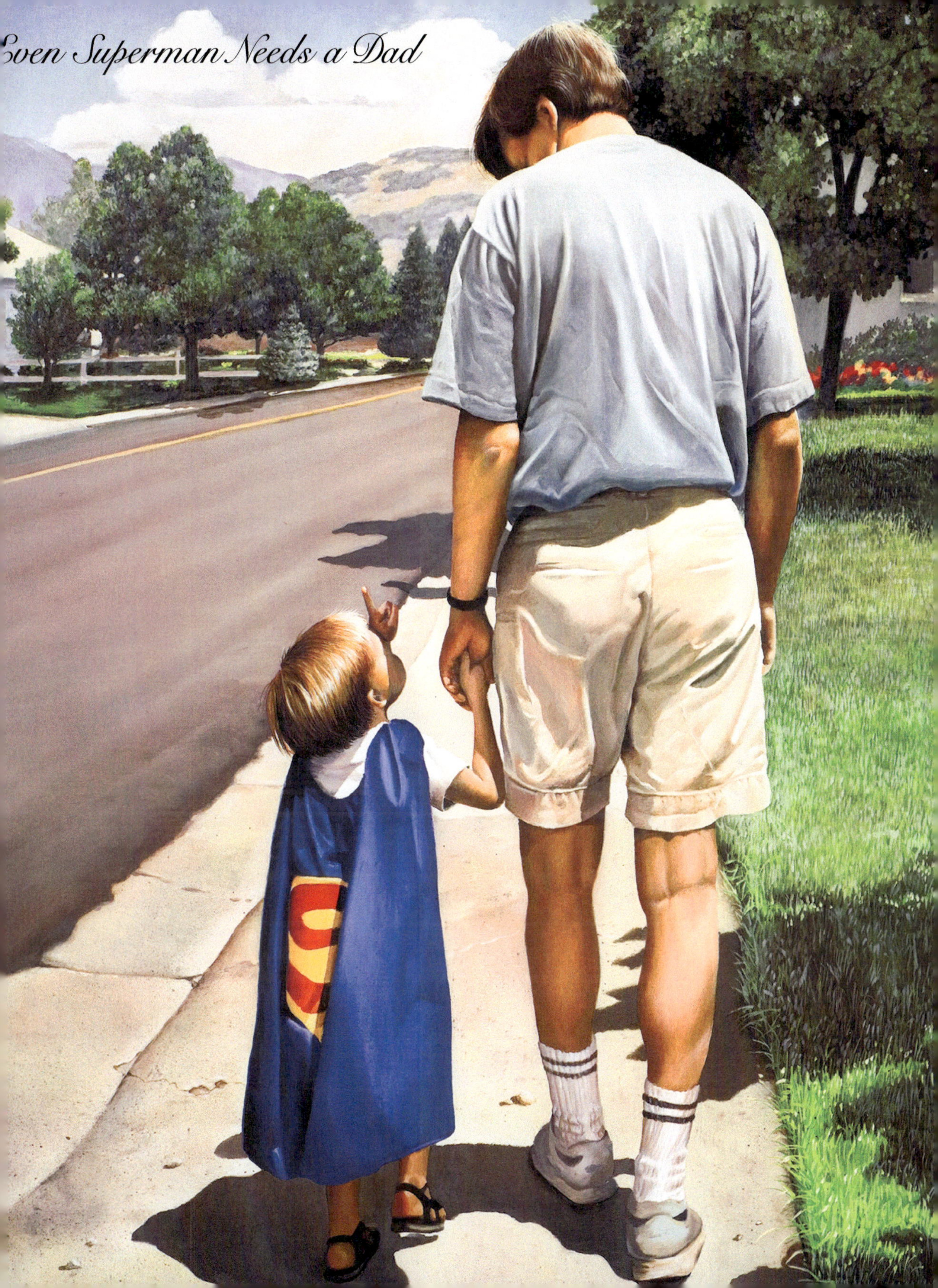

After the success of "Hair Fairies," Liz planned to paint a series on fairies—fairies who steal car keys, forget to put the cap back on the toothpaste, and discard socks in the dryer. "My ultimate goal was to be picked up as a Greenwich Workshop artist like Jim Christensen, who had become a living legend with his fantasy art," Liz says. "But after two years out of the market I couldn't start at the top. When I mentioned to Bucky the possibility of contacting my old friend Dan May of the May Galleries and telling him of my return to art as a fantasy artist, Bucky suggested an easier route would be to return to art through Frameworks. He pointed out that Frameworks and Repartee Galleries were franchises of the Connecticut-based Greenwich Workshop. With Bucky named as a distributor of Greenwich, Liz stood a good chance of being picked up as a Greenwich Workshop artist if her works were displayed in Frameworks. Liz agreed. She contacted photographer Jim Sherman and arranged for a photo shoot of models dressed as fairies. She knew she wanted to pursue fantasy art and was excited for the challenge.

Painting Joseph

Everything moved forward like clockwork until the Sunday Steevun brought his fiancée, Tami, home for dinner. Tami had put together a CD for Steevun's younger brother, Bryun, who was serving a mission in New Hampshire and feeling rather homesick. Steevun insisted that Liz sit down and listen to the Mormon pop music Tami had selected for the CD. With a pot roast ready to be taken from the oven and a table needing to be set, Liz thought Steevun's timing was questionable. More than that, she didn't like Mormon pop music, with the exception of Michael McLean's music, which had helped her get through the divorce. But knowing Tami would soon be joining her family, Liz stopped what she was doing and agreed to listen.

It was the lyrics of "Brothers" by popular LDS musician Kenneth Cope that captivated Liz's attention. The lyrics told of the love of Joseph Smith for his brother Hyrum. As Liz listened she thought of her sons and wept. Long after dinner was over, Liz listened to "Brothers" again and again. "That Sabbath Day," Liz recalls, "Joseph Smith seemed more real and the Church of Jesus Christ of Latter-day Saints more true."

Liz could hardly wait to learn more about Joseph Smith and paint Joseph and his brother Hyrum in Carthage Jail. "To me the Martyrdom encompasses all that Joseph's life had been," Liz says. "He and his brother sealed their testimony with their blood." Her plan was to create one painting of Joseph Smith that would one day be on the cover of the *Friend* or the *Ensign*. She never intended to rival artist Greg Olson or anyone else. She wasn't going to be a big player in religious art—she had no intention of painting anything more than the Martyrdom. Her plan was still to make a name for herself in fantasy art.

Liz telephoned photographer Jim Sherman and told him that she wanted to paint the Martyrdom. Jim had been planning for a photo shoot of models dressed as fairies and didn't understand what the Martyrdom of Joseph and Hyrum Smith had to do with fairies. He asked, "You want to paint Joseph Smith as a fairy?" "Not exactly," Liz replied. "But before we do the photo shoot I've got some work to do."

The next day Liz went to a Deseret Book store and purchased a stack of books on the life of Joseph Smith. She read *Joseph Smith and the Restoration* by Ivan J. Barrett, *Joseph Smith the Prophet* by Truman G. Madsen, and book after book by Susan Easton Black. Liz had an insatiable thirst for knowledge as what had been dormant in her religious life began to awaken. Liz read aloud to her daughter Jenifer and even to her dog Sassy. Soon the study of Joseph Smith's life was a family affair.

Through reading, Liz pieced together the skeletal story of Joseph Smith, but confesses, "Everything seemed mixed up. Perhaps it was because I'm an artist. I wanted to see where Nauvoo, Kirtland, and Palmyra were located and visualize the historic events recounted in the books." Liz convinced Bucky to take her to Nauvoo. Bucky had never seen the quaint historic town and was as eager as Liz to walk the streets that Joseph Smith walked in an earlier day. But Liz's sudden and intense interest in Joseph Smith was a little overwhelming. Bucky felt like he'd been thrown into the deep end of the swimming pool as he was forced to learn more about Joseph Smith than he had ever wanted to know.

Within a few days Liz and Bucky had flown to St. Louis, rented a car, and traveled up the highway to Nauvoo. "The weather in Nauvoo was great," Liz recalls. "The streets were quiet. There was a reverent feeling in town and tourists were nowhere to be found. But it was in Carthage that my life changed forever." After seeing a film in the Carthage Visitors' Center, Liz was hopeful that the actor who portrayed Joseph Smith was the same man her photographer Jim had recommended as a perfect Joseph Smith model. She called Jim to find out, and to her delight, it was. "I suppose if Joseph Smith had shown up to portray himself," Liz says, "I still would have chosen Cliff Cole over the real thing. Watching Cliff portray Joseph Smith was thrilling, but didn't come close to my experience in the upstairs bedroom of the Carthage Jail. I tried to visualize the Martyrdom and was filled with emotion. I left the room convinced that it would be a sacred privilege to paint the last moments of the life of Joseph and Hyrum Smith."

Finding Joseph and Hyrum

"Upon returning to Utah, I asked my photographer to contact Cliff Cole and see if he would be willing to be my Joseph Smith model," Liz says. "I then contacted personnel at the Church History Museum and asked about the death masks of Joseph and Hyrum Smith. I was told that I could take a replica of the death masks on loan for twelve weeks. I was told to wear gloves when using the masks because they are made of untreated plaster."

In the confines of her home, Liz studied the death masks. Of particular interest was the death mask of Hyrum Smith. "I wanted to visualize clearly his face before I selected a Hyrum model," Liz says. "One morning between being asleep and awake—a type of dream state—I saw a man who looked very familiar to me. He looked at me face to face, then turned to the side to show his profile, then turned to the other side to show the same. His bone structure was almost identical to Hyrum's death mask." Liz told Bucky about the man and together they concluded that he was the man in their stake who drove a green Jaguar, Richard Wilson, the owner of Wilson Diamonds in Provo. Liz telephoned Richard and asked him if he would portray Hyrum Smith in a photo shoot. "As it so happens, I have just returned from Nauvoo," Richard said. "On the trip my children said, 'Dad you look just like Hyrum Smith.'"

Liz next looked for a place that had the same floor plan as Carthage Jail. "To my surprise I discovered that the nursery in my ward meetinghouse had the correct dimensions," Liz says. "Even the windows and door were in the right place. The only thing missing was the fireplace."

"On the day of the photo shoot in October 1994," Liz says, "Cliff arrived at my front door. He looked really big to me. He stands about 6'4" and has a definite presence. Until he spoke I felt that Joseph Smith had just walked into my living room. He was completely disarming and wonderfully nice. I came back to reality, handed him his costume, and told him to change in the spare bedroom. A few minutes later Cliff walked out my back door and down the decks. As far as I was concerned, he was Joseph again.

"It's funny how clothes can make the man," Liz says. "Cliff stayed in character and called for a prayer before we filmed the final farewell of Joseph Smith and his family in my backyard. Everything went like clockwork after the prayer. There was no need for any retake. I had never begun a photo shoot with prayer before nor had I attempted to paint anything that had the potential to stir emotion like the farewell of Joseph and his family. I had painted ducks and fairies, but this was different."

After the photo shoot in the backyard, Liz and her group moved to the nursery room in the ward meetinghouse to film the Martyrdom. As they set up the room Liz felt nervous, even panicky. She wondered if Heavenly Father really wanted her to paint the final scene of the lives of Joseph and Hyrum Smith. Sensing her doubts, her son Steevun looked at her and said, "You need a prayer."

Liz retorted, "We've already prayed."

Steevun advised, "Ask Heavenly Father to tell you what to do. You need help directing the scene. You need to be calm." Liz felt guilty for her arrogance and knew Steevun was right.

After the prayer Cliff came up to Liz and said, "You seem to be having trouble. Do you need help?" Cliff became the director and Liz moved to the background. Cliff got everyone in position, had the photographer adjust the camera, and said, "Action!" Cliff and Richard Wilson went to the door of the nursery.

"When I saw Cliff and Richard push against the door," Liz says, "it was as if I could see the energy of the mob pushing against the door from the other side, for Cliff and Richard used all their might to keep the door closed. When Richard fell to the floor, he said, 'I'm a dead man.' The scene was so shocking! I had a

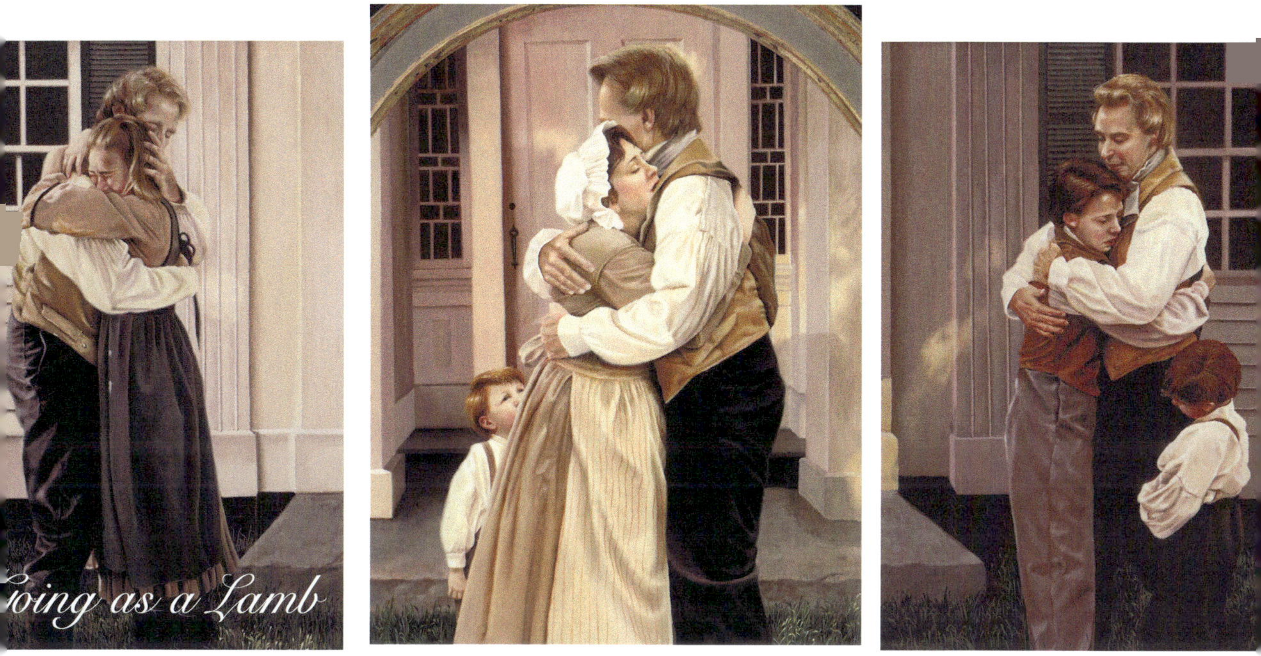

hard time not stepping into it. Cliff walked over and scooped Richard up in his arms. There was no other way to convey the love of the brothers Joseph and Hyrum. With tears pouring from his eyes and falling onto the face of Richard, Cliff said, 'O, my dear brother, Hyrum.' As Richard lay on the floor Cliff went to the window and cried out, 'O Lord, My God.' No one moved. The photographer said, 'Cut.' There were no retakes. What I had witnessed was the most spiritual experience of my life to that point. Everyone in the room felt the same thing. At that moment I knew that I could never return to painting fairies."

After the photo shoot Cliff said to Liz, "What you are doing is of the Lord, because all of the feelings that I had in Nauvoo came rushing back." Cliff explained that when he was asked to portray Joseph Smith in films to be shown in the Carthage and Nauvoo Visitors' Centers, he was very nervous and concerned about making mistakes. Elder Loren C. Dunn of the Seventy offered to give him a blessing. In the blessing, Cliff was told that the Lord would bless him to portray the feelings and actions of Joseph Smith and that he would feel as Joseph felt—even fear at his impending death—as long as what he was doing was for the Lord. Cliff told Liz, "I know that what you are doing is of the Lord. Otherwise I wouldn't have been allowed to feel the way I did during the photo shoot."

Night had fallen and Liz was exhausted. She locked the meetinghouse and slowly started walking across the parking lot to her home. She thought back on the day's events and of a conversation she had had years ago with a friend. She had sought the friend's advice about wanting to leave wildlife art to do something new, something she could put her heart into. His advice was simple: "Paint what you know." As Liz reflected on the events of the day and how powerful and wonderful yet vulnerable she felt, she recognized that she knew these things long before that day. She had been raised in the Mormon Church and had never questioned the truthfulness of any of its history or doctrine because she knew it was true in her heart. Liz was at peace, for she had come home.

Due to the sacred nature of the photo shoot and the hours spent painting "O My Dear Brother Hyrum," Liz anticipated that her

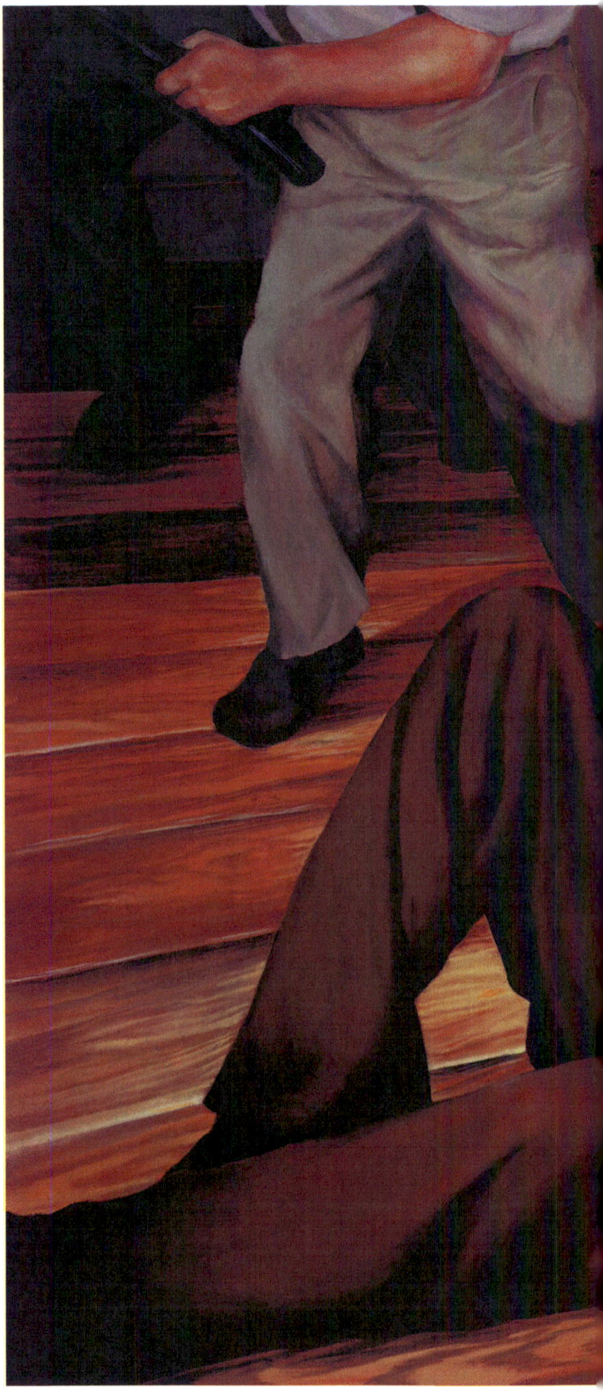

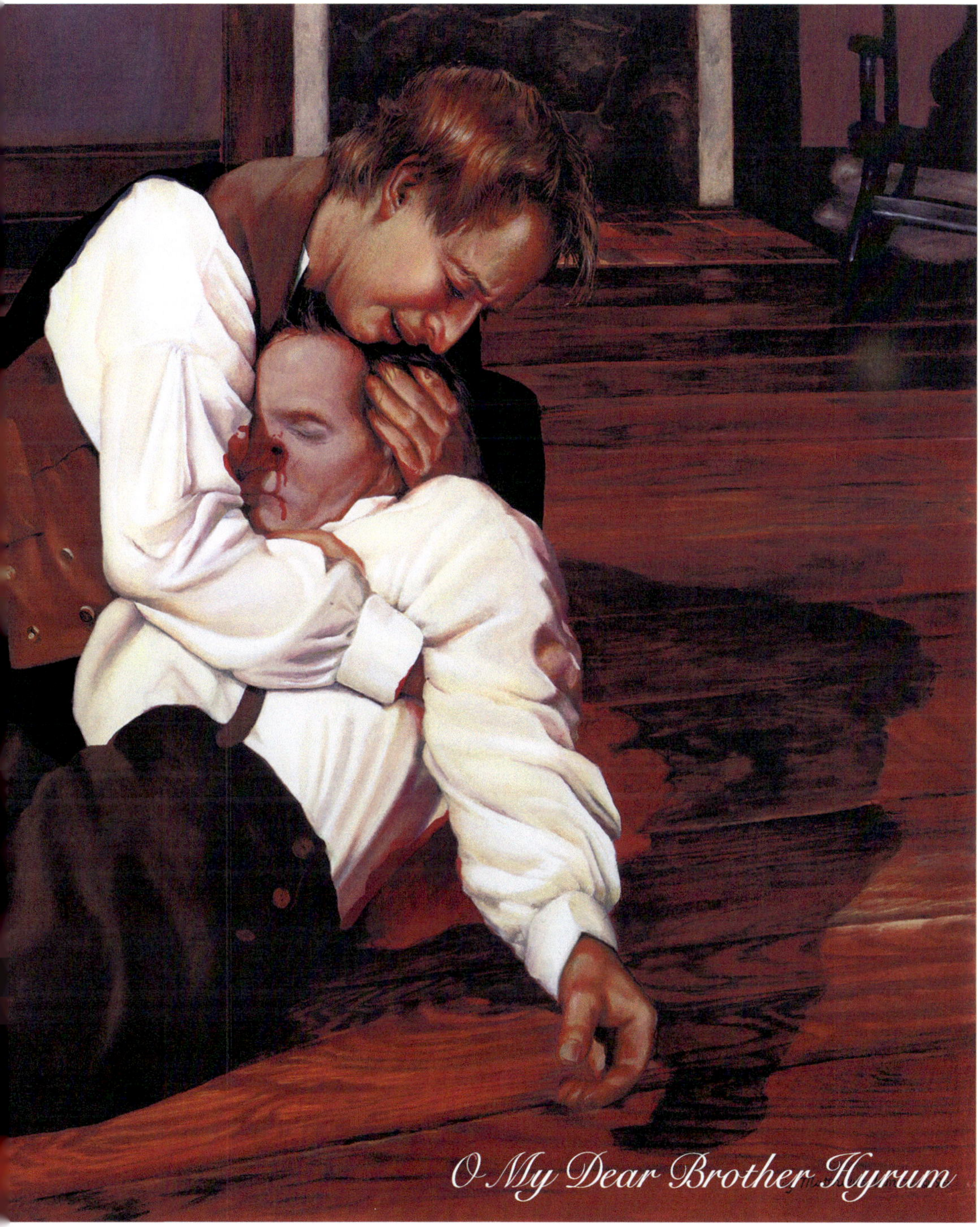

O My Dear Brother Hyrum

portrayal of the Martyrdom would be a blockbuster and customers would clamor for prints at the galleries. She saw the original painting as a hotly contested item among prospective buyers. However, when she spoke to a wealthy friend about having the first right of refusal on the painting, certain the deal was a slam dunk, the friend said, "I couldn't hang something so sorrowful in my house. I have little children." Every potential buyer Liz approached had the same reaction. They couldn't see what Liz saw—the painting represented Joseph Smith rejoicing that he was leaving this life triumphant for having sealed his testimony with his blood.

Although Liz was deeply disappointed that a buyer hadn't come forward, she wasn't discouraged—one of her greatest hallmarks. She pushed forward and painted "Restoration." Recalling that painting, Liz says, "I struggled most of the day to paint Joseph's face correctly by looking at photographs. As silly as it may seem I was afraid to hold the death mask for fear I might drop it. I kept it covered with a black cloth. It wasn't until late in the afternoon that I took the mask in my hand. I spent an hour or so fixing the trouble spots I'd wrestled with all day. I set the mask down, stepped back, and looked at the painting. I had painted a near look alike to Joseph's face. The spirit in the room was palpable. I felt as if someone had wrapped me in a warm blanket and I had melted into its folds. My husband returned home from work, poked his head in the studio, and then shut the door abruptly. I stayed in the studio for what seemed like hours. I didn't want to do anything that would cause the feeling to end."

Later that evening Liz asked Bucky why he hadn't come in the studio and talked to her. He said, "I wasn't supposed to be there. The Spirit was so powerful in the room I felt as if you were being taught a lesson of sorts. I felt like you were being prepared for something."

Liz says, "I understood Bucky's feeling but didn't have words to describe it." What she did know was that Bucky understood her need to paint the Restoration and his role to encourage her. Liz often remarks, "My success is his success. The paintings of Joseph Smith would never have been painted without Bucky."

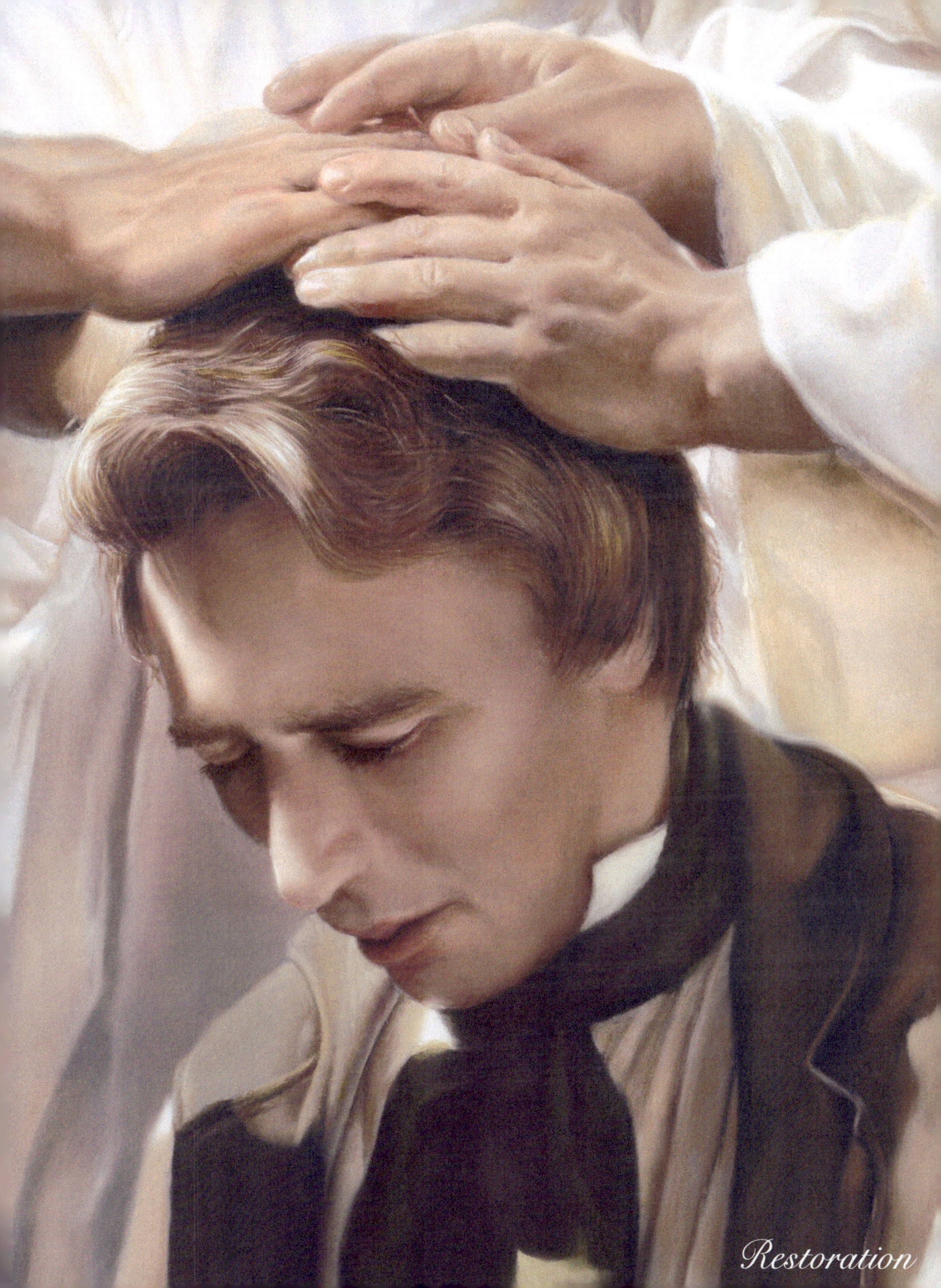

Restoration

While Emma Sleeps

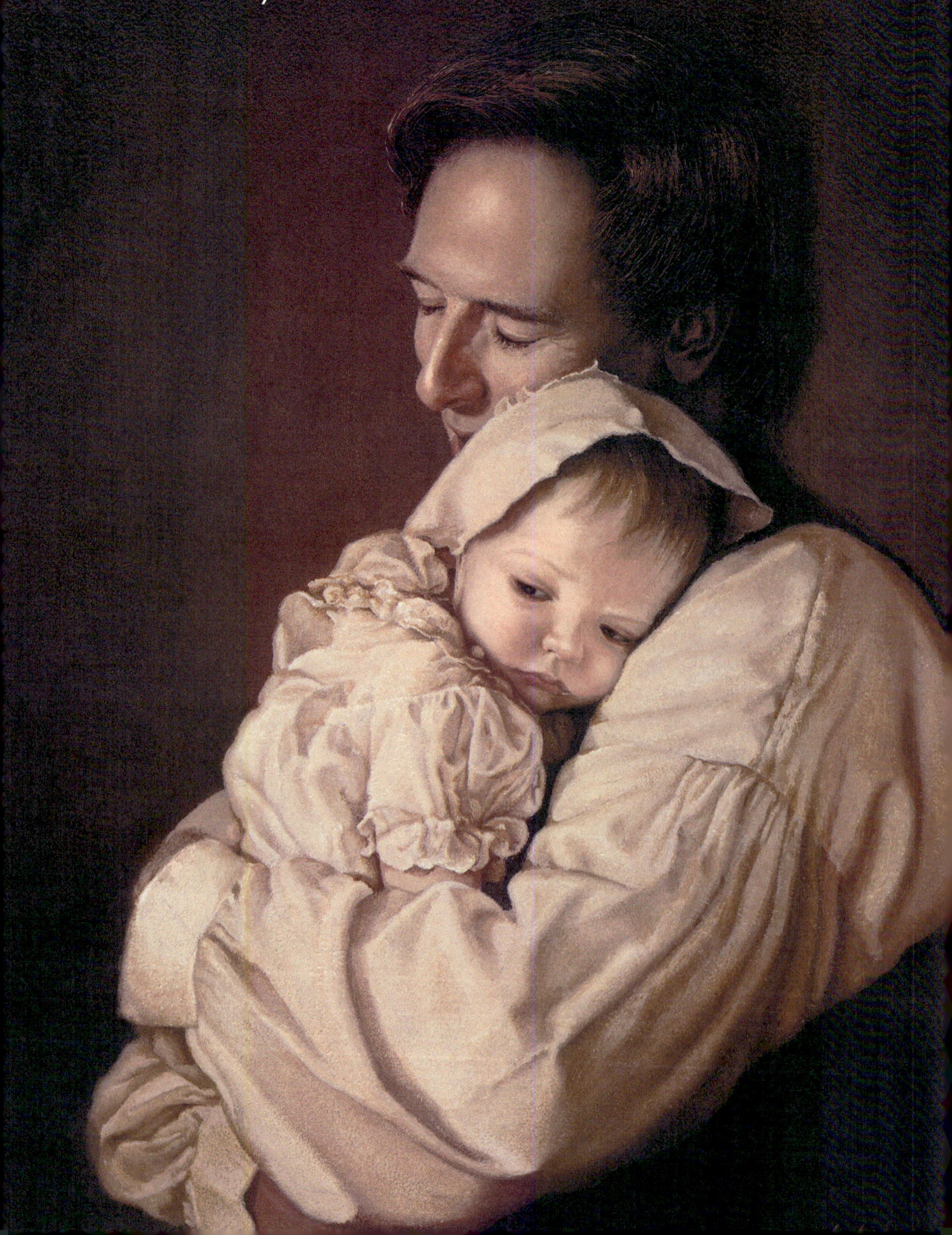

The Price of Painting

It was Bucky's support—financially, emotionally, and professionally—that made these paintings possible. For example, while Liz was completing the painting "While Emma Sleeps," a buyer offered 6,500 dollars for the original. Knowing that the sale was all but complete, Liz made travel arrangements to Palmyra, New York, and Kirtland, Ohio, for herself and about six others, which included the photographer and models. She booked airplane flights, hotel rooms, and rental cars. The advance cost of 5,795 dollars was charged to Bucky's American Express Card with the assumption that the sale of "While Emma Sleeps" would cover all costs. The night before Liz and her group left for the airport, Bucky got a phone call from the gallery informing him that the buyer of "While Emma Sleeps" had pulled out. When Bucky told Liz, she broke into tears. "Should we cancel?" she asked. Without hesitation Bucky said, "Absolutely not!" The trip went as scheduled. On the day the American Express bill came, the gallery called Bucky to inform him that "While Emma Sleeps" had just sold. Prayers of thanksgiving were offered.

"This experience allowed me to build a foundation of faith," Liz says. "Bucky and I were rarely given easy outcomes, but our faith grew by leaps and bounds when we were put to the test. Now, twenty-two years later, little has changed. The cost of trips and photo shoots have, at times, been staggering. The expense of photographers, lighting equipment, wardrobe, makeup, props, and travel accommodations can be prohibitive. It is not like the days of Norman Rockwell when an artist could go out his front door, find a neighborhood kid with the right look, and pay him a quarter to sit for twenty minutes in a specific pose. Being an artist today is expensive. Then there are the incidentals like paying union wages to four Palestinians to carry a generator fifty feet on the Mount of Olives or paying four times the amount agreed upon to rent a 'Jesus' boat at night on the Sea of Galilee because they forgot to charge for the hardship their business had suffered due to a recent economic

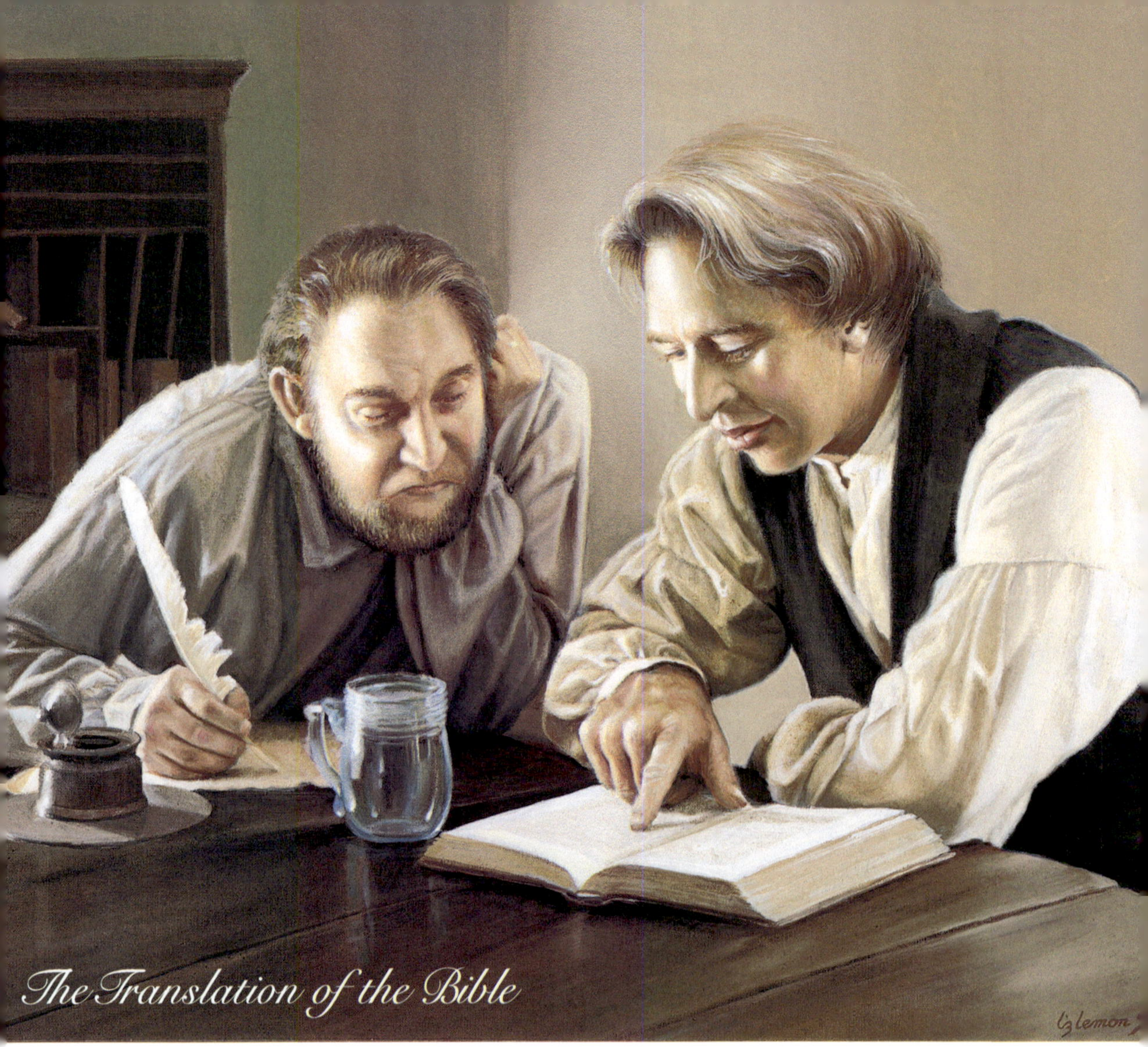

downturn or the emergency plane fare to allow someone in our group to fly home to deal with a family crisis."

In a real sense Bucky has been the executive producer of Liz's religious art works. He handles the financial cares and only on rare occasions says, "I hope we can pay for this." He never says, "Let's do it a cheaper way." Bucky trusts Liz, sits quietly in the background, and beams with delight as he watches her orchestrate photo shoots. He's even been willing to model as Sidney Rigdon in "The Translation of the Bible," a mobber in "Majesty in Chains," and a wise man in "The Holy Men." Perhaps Bucky's willingness to support Liz is best illustrated in the May 1995 photo shoot called "Nauvoo Days."

For that day Liz needed scrap—photos used as references in painting—to create scenarios with a lot of people in places like Nauvoo and Kirtland. She telephoned a few neighbors and ward members to ask if they would dress-up like pioneers and spend a day in a local park being filmed. The response was overwhelming. Liz contacted Kathryn Warner, a professional costume mistress, and asked if she could supply costumes. Kathryn arranged for roughly three hundred costumes, and ward members supplied over a hundred dresses, aprons, petticoats, bloomers, and day bonnets. Carol Patterson and Riley Jeffrey, professional tailors, sewed another fifty ensembles of shirts, pants, and hats for boys and men. Who funded Nauvoo Days? Bucky, of course.

Hoping to help defray Bucky's costs, Liz contacted her bishop to see if Nauvoo Days could be the ward summer social in hopes of subsidizing the expenses with the budget allotted to the activities committee for parties. The answer was no, but as Liz put it, "You never know until you ask." The bishop did agree that Nauvoo Days could be the ward summer social, but would not subsidize any costs—not quite what Liz was hoping for.

On Nauvoo Days, hundreds of people played in the park while Jim Sherman photographed impromptu scenes hour after hour. Horses and buggies supplied by Fenton Quinn provided countless rides for children around the park. A greased pig chase, and old-fashioned swings with thirty-foot ropes kept children and parents busy for hours. Three-legged races, gunnysack races, quilting, stickball, hoops, horseback riding, log-sawing, and tables filled with Sherolyn Medford's homemade bread were crowd favorites. "Special guests Kenneth Cope, whose music 'Brothers' was the inspiration for the 'Martyrdom' painting, and Joseph Paur of *Rigoletto* fame from Los Angeles were the icing on a perfect day," Liz says. "One little boy, Jason, Cooper followed Cliff around all day and tried to mirror his every action. When Cliff Cole put his hands in his pocket so did young Jason. The photographer captured the scene on camera."

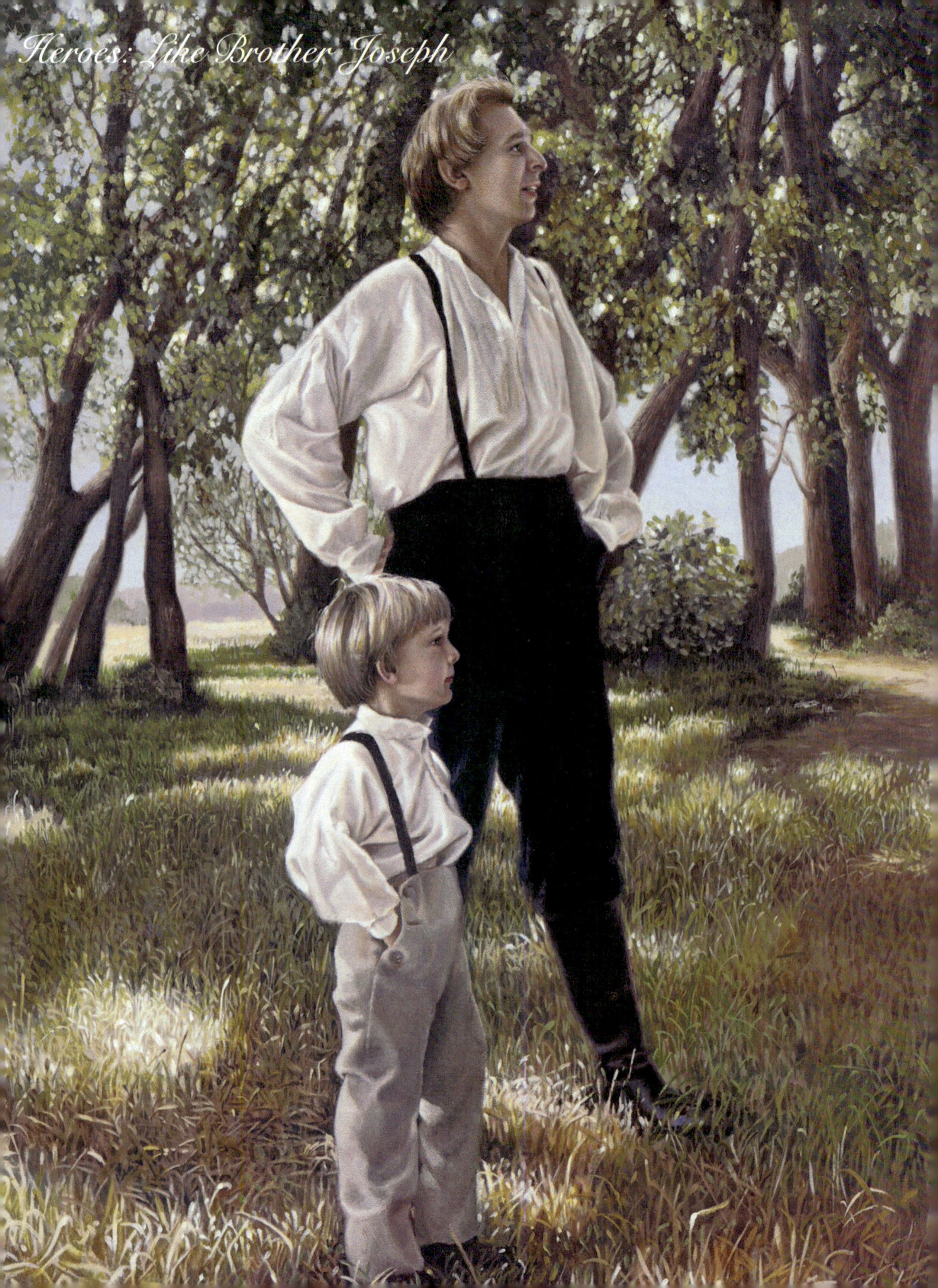

Heroes: Like Brother Joseph

As Nauvoo Days ended, Liz caught her breath and tears began to fall. "I can't believe so many people wanted to be a part of this," she said to Bucky. "So many friends and neighbors contributed their time and talents to make this day special. How will we ever thank them?" That night Bucky and Liz knelt by their bed with humble hearts and thanked Heavenly Father for the wonderful day. They both felt there would be many wonderful days like this one—maybe not with four hundred people—but days filled with great joy. They knew that other artists had painted events in the life of Joseph Smith, but there had never been a massive event like Nauvoo Days with the specific purpose to have a woman explore Joseph's feelings and those of his followers on canvas. What Liz was doing was groundbreaking in Mormon art and she wasn't about to stop. In looking back, Liz says, "This was a happy time for me. I still felt like a newlywed and had available to me unlimited discretionary funds."

"Then came my Kirtland extravaganza," Liz recalls. "I rented the Kirtland Temple for the whole day and took my group with me for a large sum. Any man other than Bucky would have grown feathers over that kind of spending. Bucky believed in the project and what I was trying to do. He was willing to risk his all for my photo shoots. He smiled when cars driving on the street in front of the Kirtland Temple stopped and passengers came running inside the temple to see what appeared to be Christ." Bucky even paid the fare for Liz and her models, photographer, and entourage to travel to the British Isles. The cost was exorbitant, but Bucky believed in Liz and supported her however he could.

Bringing Joseph to Life

As more paintings on the life of Joseph Smith were placed on canvas, Liz became aware of a nagging flaw—the flesh was "too hot," too orange in hue. She telephoned several artists and university professors to ask about their technique for painting flesh. Their responses weren't very helpful. She petitioned Heavenly Father for direction on how to paint flesh and on who could teach her. It wasn't until Liz attended a gala event for LDS artists held at the BYU Museum of Art that the answer came. At the event, artist Lynn Millman-Winegar passed out brochures promoting an upcoming workshop by Frank Covino. The mere mention of his name garnered snide comments from other artists who viewed him in the same category as a circus barker. As Liz looked at the brochure announcing the Covino workshop, she saw beautifully rendered flesh. She asked the artist seated next to her, "Are you going?"

He replied, "You'd never catch me there." Liz joined him and others in berating Covino, but for the next several days she couldn't get his rendering of flesh out of her mind.

"I didn't see the workshop as an answer to my prayers," Liz says. "I was too prideful. I argued with the Spirit, saying, 'I can't go. I can't be seen in Covino's workshop.' I finally concluded that I could go but not until the lights were down and I could find a place to stand in the back of the room. An usher took me in and pointed to my seat. After sitting down I looked up at the screen and saw Covino's rendition of an old woman in a chair with a cigarette in her mouth. I thought, *The skin tone and texture on the woman's face and hands are perfect. This is where Heavenly Father wants me to be. I can learn from Covino and don't care who sees me in this class.* When the lights came up I saw most of the artists who had spoken disparagingly of Covino at the Museum of Art."

Liz listened intently as Covino said, "I don't understand why you Mormon artists are not painting your heritage. You paint a painting here and there but no one in your Church has painted a body of work of the early Saints and the history of your people." Even then Liz didn't take the challenge; she didn't see her paintings as a part of anything epic.

Years later, Liz was asked to be the keynote speaker at Tuacahn, a beautiful facility for the arts in the majestic red rock canyons of southern Utah. After delivering her remarks, a well-known fellow artist said to her, "I enjoyed your remarks but you need to be careful and not tell anyone else that you studied under Frank Covino. It discredits your work."

Liz's amazement quickly turned to anger. "How can I possibly deny the source that so freely taught me principles that I couldn't find anywhere else?" Liz said. "To do so would be more than ungrateful, not just to Covino, but to my Heavenly Father as well."

"The Premier Artist on the Life of Joseph Smith"

With more paintings leaving the easel and sales at the galleries increasing, Bucky wanted to hire a publicist to advance what Liz was calling, "Impressions of a Prophet." Liz suggested Janita Anderson for the position. Years before, Liz had worked with Janita, publicist for the Dinosaur Museum on the BYU campus, and thought it would be a good match. She was hired and "Impressions" was soon a hot topic in the LDS art market. First came a feature article in the *Daily Herald.* This was followed by word of "Impressions" moving from a local stage to a national level in a matter of months. By the time Liz had completed ten paintings in the "Impressions" series, the publicist and other personnel at Repartee Gallery were asking if she would write an illustrative book about the Prophet Joseph Smith.

"My talents do not reside in the literary arts," Liz says, "yet I was intrigued with the idea and telephoned Steevun." "Who would you like to write the book?" Steevun asked.

"Susan Easton Black," Liz said.

Steevun replied, "You don't want her—she's a woman. You need Gerald N. Lund." Lund had written the popularized series The Work and the Glory. Liz did not want a fictionalized account of the Prophet Joseph. Liz and Steevun discussed several other Church writers until Steevun, in frustration, said, "Fine, use Susan."

The next day, Liz received a phone call: "Hello, this is Susan Easton Black." Liz thought it was Else Visick, the secretary at Repartee Gallery, pretending to be Susan at Steevun's request.

Flippantly, Liz replied, "Sure you are."

Again Susan insistently said, "This is Dr. Black from BYU." She went on to say that one of her students had handed her a small print of "Even Superman Needs a Dad" and had written on the back of the print, "You'll want to meet Liz Swindle—she's becoming the premier artist on the life of Joseph Smith."

"The timing of the phone call was uncanny," Liz says. "I agreed to meet Susan at Frameworks in the University Mall."

Susan recalls their first meeting: "It was easy to spot Liz Lemon Swindle at Frameworks. She looked like a hippie with a paintbrush holding back her hair. It was an awkward meeting for me until I was shown one of Liz's paintings of Joseph Smith. There wasn't just emotion in her work, there was grandeur. To me Liz was no longer the hippie or farm girl from Perry, Utah, who happened to pick up a paint brush—she was an inspired artist driven to share her faith in Joseph Smith's prophetic calling with the world."

In 1998, Liz and Susan collaborated on *Joseph Smith: Impressions of a Prophet*, published by Deseret Book. The book, featuring thirty-seven paintings of Joseph Smith, was an instant success with multiple printings within the first three months. But the book couldn't compete with the "Joseph Smith Show" in Salt Lake City that featured Liz's original paintings of the Prophet Joseph. The show was held in the main entry/foyer of the Joseph Smith Memorial Building (the remodeled Hotel Utah). Crowds waiting to enter the "Joseph Smith Show" extended out the door of the memorial building and down the block past the north side of the Salt Lake Temple. It is estimated that over fifteen thousand people viewed Liz's original paintings over one weekend. They were slow to move along, for many were overcome by the artistic renditions of the Prophet Joseph. Among the attendees were President Gordon B. Hinckley and members of the Quorum of the Twelve Apostles.

Following the show, both Liz and Susan spent many a Saturday at book signings where lines were often backed up and flowing out of the door. At one such signing, Elder David B. Haight of the Twelve waited patiently in line to meet the duo and to purchase a book for his wife. Upon meeting them he asked, "Are you the Black-Swindle team? I can't come home without your book; I think my wife, Ruby, likes you best of all."

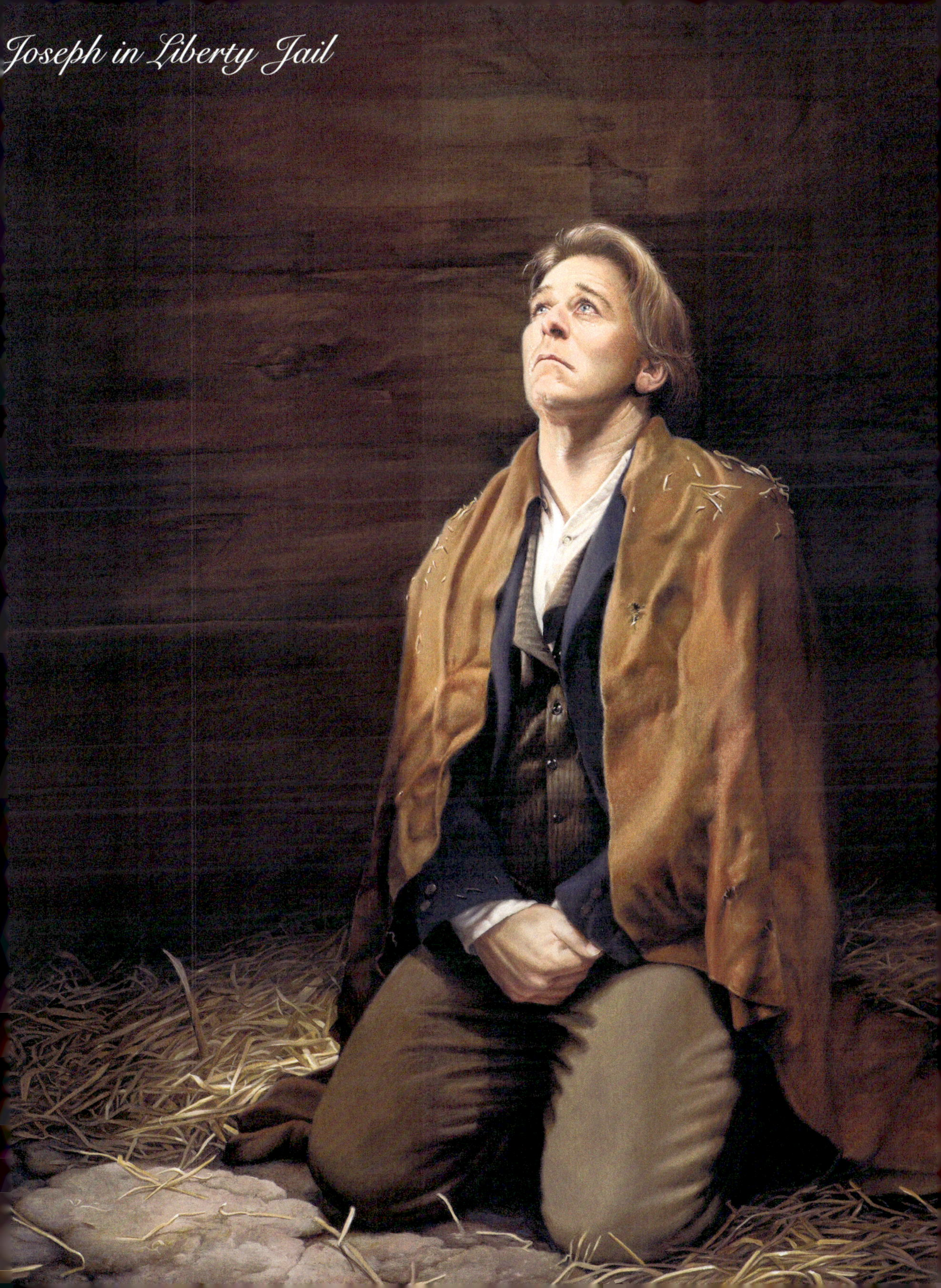

Joseph in Liberty Jail

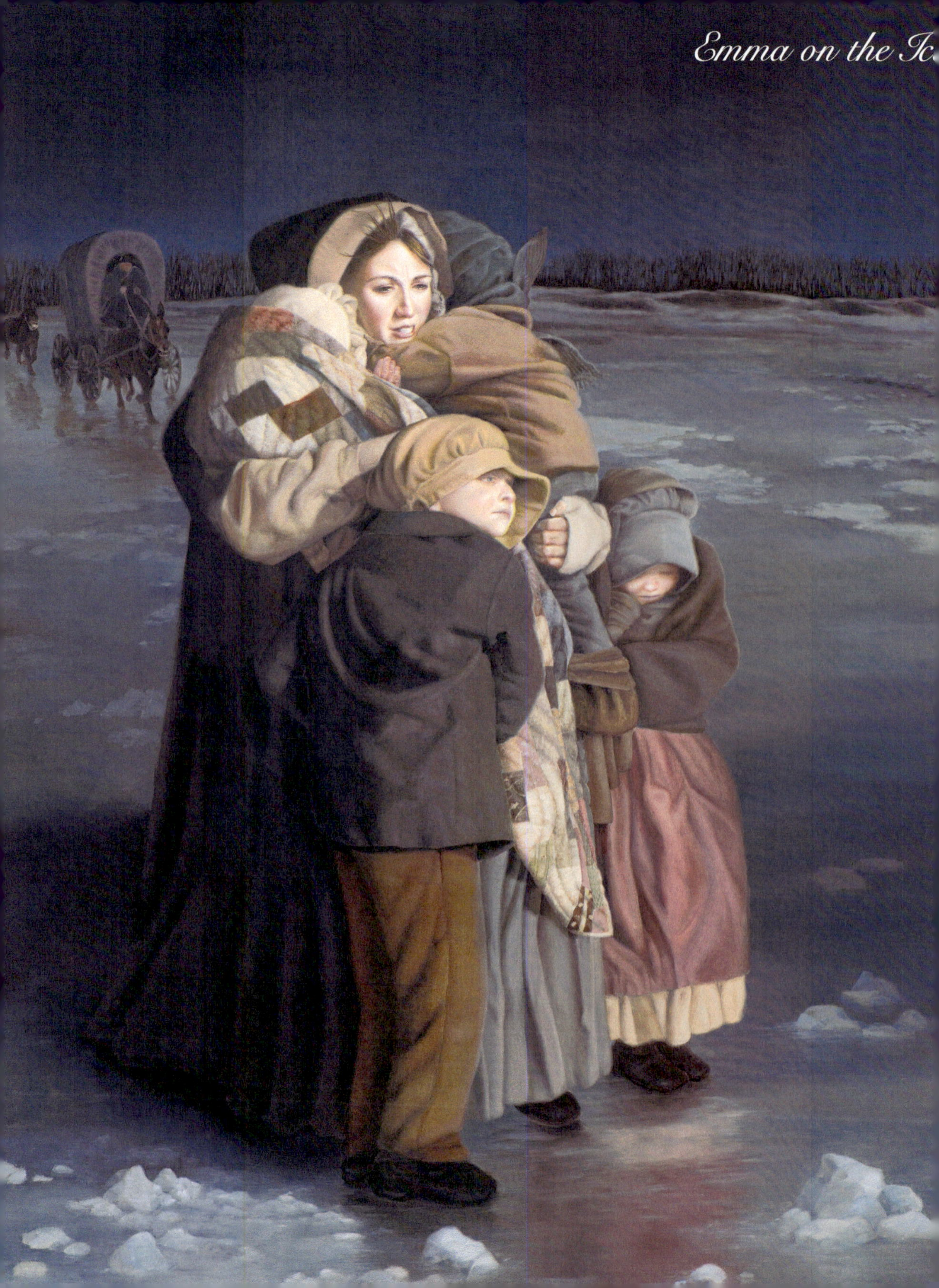

Emma on the Ic

From this point on, Liz's paintings of Joseph Smith were boxed up and sent across the country to be displayed in LDS visitors' centers in Independence, Missouri; Nauvoo, Illinois; and Washington, D.C. Among the thousands who viewed her paintings, many exclaimed, "I've never seen anything like this." As the tour of paintings was nearing an end, the state of Missouri commissioned Liz to paint the Mormon experience in Missouri and gave her total autonomy to create one or more paintings. She painted "Joseph in Liberty Jail" and "Emma on the Ice." In preparation for these paintings, Liz read Elder Neal A. Maxwell's book, *But for a Small Moment.* Liz was so inspired by his book, that she called Neal A Maxwell's secretary, Susan, in hopes of sending Elder Maxwell a print of her painting "Joseph in Liberty Jail" to thank him for his inspiration. Susan telephoned Liz and said, "Instead of mailing the print, Elder Maxwell would like you to come in and meet with him. You may bring the print with you then." Liz planned on a short visit with the Apostle, but after forty-five minutes, she found it hard to concentrate, afraid she was holding up something more important. During their visit, Elder Maxwell asked what projects she had planned to do once she completed her paintings on the life of Joseph Smith. When Liz told him she planned to do a series on the life of Jesus Christ, he expressed profound interest and asked if she would consult with him as a friend on the project, meeting together frequently to discuss Liz's paintings. From this point on, Liz met with Elder Maxwell every three months for four years. Elder Maxwell hung the painting "Joseph in Liberty Jail" in his office and would refer people to it when discussing their trials with him. When Elder Maxwell passed away, his wife hung it in their home.

Liz was invited to attend the unveiling ceremony of her paintings in the rotunda of the capitol building in Jefferson City, Missouri. "It was a thrill for me to watch as Governor Carnahan of Missouri unveiled my commissioned paintings 'Joseph in Liberty Jail' and 'Emma on the Ice,'" Liz says. Following the unveiling, the governor presented Elder Hugh Pinnock of the Seventy with an apology for the Extermination Order issued by Governor Lilburn W. Boggs in 1838. "This was one of those truly great moments in life where everything seems to connect," Liz says, "where my contribution became an important part of something big. I couldn't believe that I was in the capital of Missouri as part of an apology for the Extermination Order."

The unveiling ceremony was followed by many invitations and requests for Liz to speak about her art and her experience in creating "Impressions." "The first time I was asked to speak on 'Impressions of a Prophet' was in Bountiful at Camille Jensen's ward," Liz recalls. "During the fifty-eight-minute drive to Bountiful, I cried the entire time. Bearing my testimony was scary back then, and speaking was over the top. I didn't mind painting portraits of Joseph, but I did mind having to speak about them." However, it didn't take long before Liz became a pro at public speaking. It was not an unusual month for her to spend days away from home speaking throughout the country about Joseph Smith and showing visuals of her paintings. One month alone she spoke at seventeen different firesides. "This was becoming my new norm and way of life," Liz says. "One of the memorial firesides was in the east, where I was picked up in a limousine at the JFK International Airport. I wished then my father had been alive to see me step into a limousine—and all this because I was painting the life of Joseph Smith.

"I'll never forget the night that Susan, Kenneth Cope, and I spoke to the youth in my stake," Liz says. "The cultural hall was packed. As President Summerfeldt was introducing us, I looked over at Susan and noticed that she didn't have any notes. I wondered how she could possibly speak without notes. I panicked for her and prayed she'd remember all she had prepared. Then, without a hiccup, Susan stood at the pulpit without a single piece of paper and held the congregation mesmerized for thirty minutes."

With hundreds of talks behind her, Liz can now walk in "cold turkey" in any public setting and do the same. She has spoken at the General Authorities Wives' Luncheon and sat at the same table with Sister Hinckley, Sister Monson, and Sister Maxwell. She has dined with Sister Maxwell again and again. Who had once been the misfit girl from Perry is no more—Liz moves gracefully in a different sphere.

Painting the Savior

As her work on Joseph Smith began to wind down, the name of Liz Lemon Swindle was spoken of as if in neon lights. She saw herself having "moved in the LDS art community from a possible B-list to an A-list of artists. Collectors were coming out of the walls and so were competitors." Copycat artists were trying to replicate her work. In the wake of growing fame came criticism, surprisingly from the LDS art community—"She's only an illustrator," "She has no talent," and worst of all, "She married Bucky to advance her career." Liz will always be grateful for fellow artist Bob Marshall who countered, "Liz Lemon Swindle will always be known as the Joseph Smith artist of the LDS Church." But Marshall's comment did little to soften the blows Liz felt.

While feeling sorry for herself on the artistic front, Liz started to become discouraged on the economic front as well. Liz took issue with living in a 2,200-square-foot home on a road with a yellow strip running down the middle. During this period, she visited a friend who had just purchased a massive home in Arizona. "I'm happy for her," Liz said to Bucky. "She deserves that beautiful house. Am I ever going to get a big home or must I wait for the mansion promised on the other side?" Bucky put his hands on her shoulders and said, "This doesn't play well with you. Choose today if you want to serve Heavenly Father with everything you've got. Heavenly Father is happy with all you've done. We can get a bigger house and forget this whole thing." Liz recalls, "His straightforward comment caused me to reevaluate my situation and what I really wanted out of life. I determined then and there that I wouldn't look back. Whether or not my paintings sold or no matter what envious artists had to say, I would not give up the faithful ground I had gained. I would not return to being a 'Sunday Mormon' or painting an occasional religious piece. I was willing to move forward with religious art, come what may."

This time Liz had no difficulty in choosing the next subject. For years she had mused about her paintings of Joseph Smith being a preparation for painting the life and times of Jesus Christ. Her feelings were confirmed when Deseret Book commissioned a Christmas card in 1999.

Liz painted the iconic, "Be It unto Me" for the Christmas card. Deseret Book executives rejected the painting that would become Liz's signature piece with the comment, "We want Mary to look more interactive with baby Jesus." In four days Liz painted "She Shall Bring Forth a Son," and still regrets the time crunch.

Knowing that Deseret Book had missed the mark and that Scott Usher, owner and proprietor of company Greenwich Workshop, a secular company, and a distributor to fifteen hundred art galleries, was coming to the Repartee Gallery in Provo, Bucky placed "Be It unto Me" in a prime location in the gallery. Liz says, "When Scott saw the painting, it nearly blew him away because Mary looked like his wife and the baby looked like his premature newborn son."

Scott asked Bucky, "Does this artist have any other works that I can review?"

Bucky said, "Funny you should ask." He showed Scott Liz's body of work on the Prophet Joseph Smith. When Scott saw that she had excelled, producing over thirty renderings, he signed Liz up that very day as a Greenwich Workshop artist. "It was like winning the Oscars," Liz says. "Greenwich only took the best and the brightest, like James Christensen and his fantasy art. Greenwich had propelled Christensen to a national level and was about to do

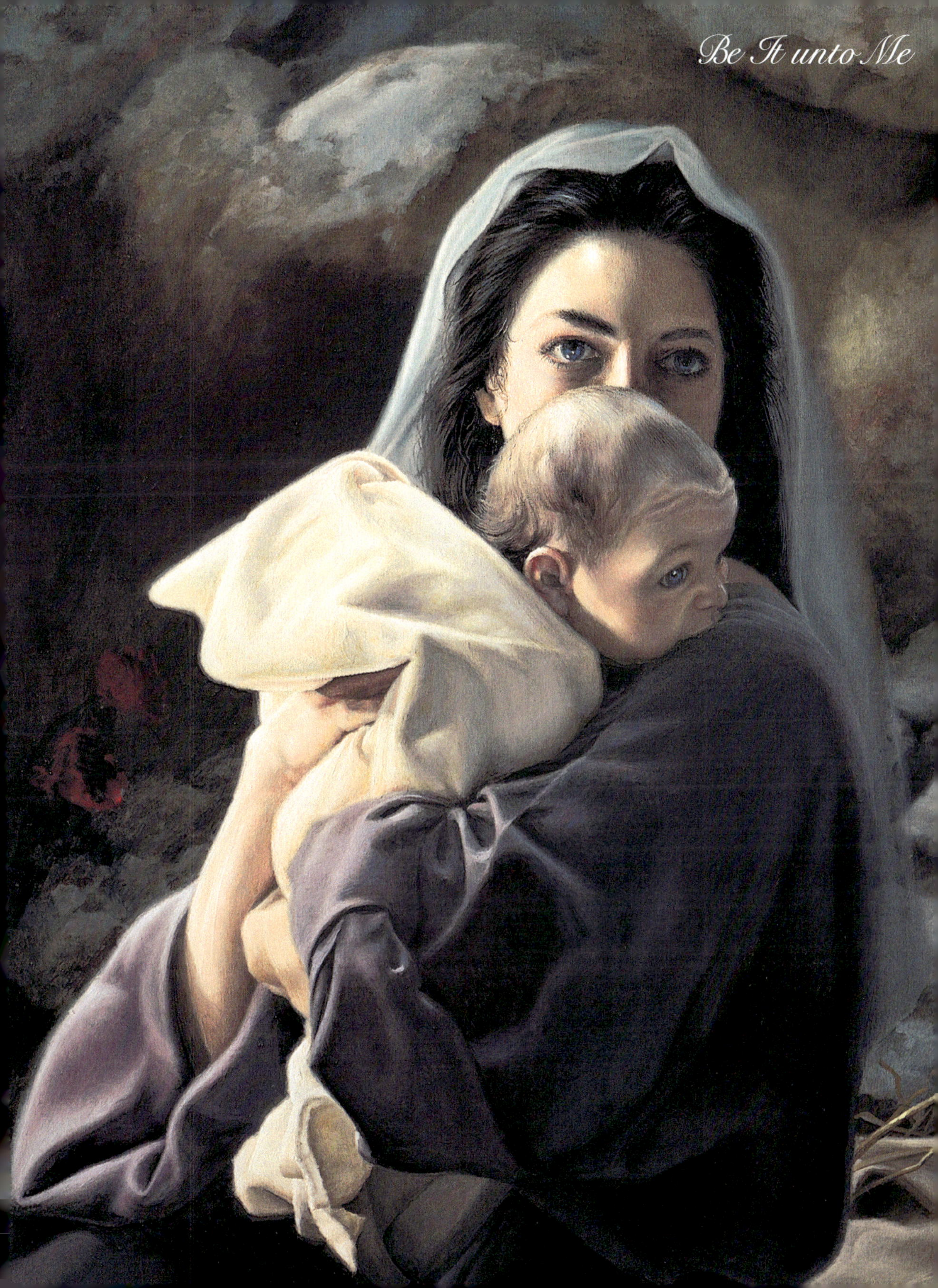

Be It unto Me

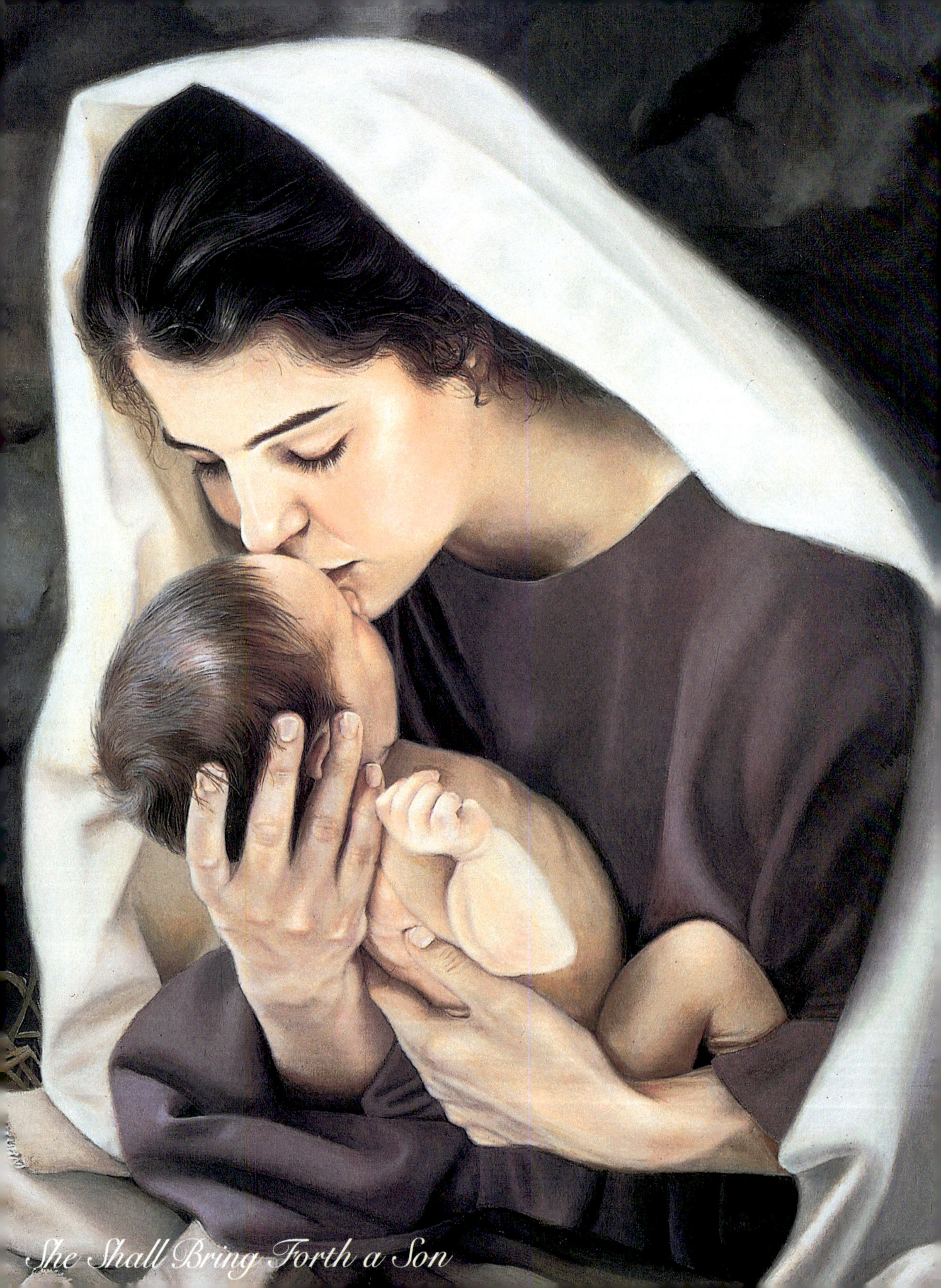

She Shall Bring Forth a Son

the same for me. Becoming a Greenwich artist was not just a huge jump up the ladder—it was the pinnacle."

Scott Usher saw Liz's work as commercially viable when "Be It unto Me" sold out in less than two months.

Knowing that her audience would expand beyond the LDS market, Liz was concerned that Greenwich would not understand how to sell her artwork to a Christian market and that they would interfere with her artistic process because they wouldn't know the Savior and would be more concerned with profits. Needing guidance, she contacted Elder Maxwell asking for a blessing for her and her team as they started "The Son of Man" project. Her team consisted of Susan Easton Black who was writing the text for their upcoming book, *Son of Man: The Early Years;* Kenneth Cope who was composing music; and Phillip, the model for the Savior. On October 15, 1999, Elder Maxwell gave Liz, Susan, and Kenneth blessings before they launched into the project.

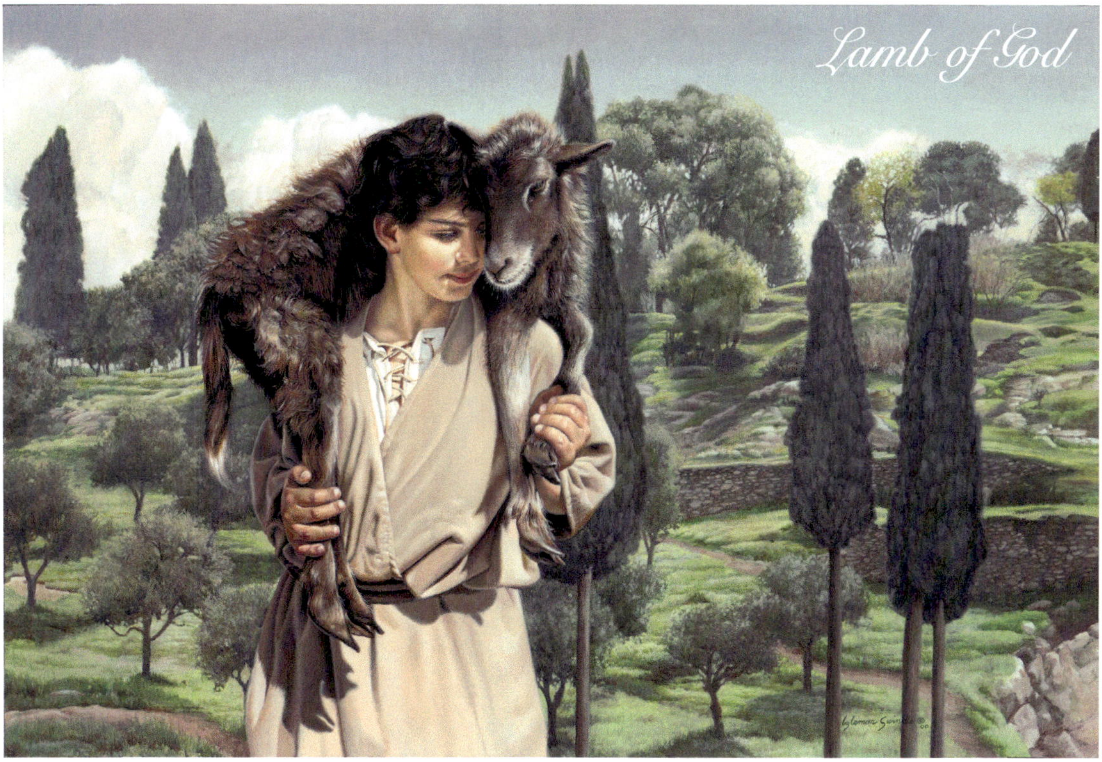

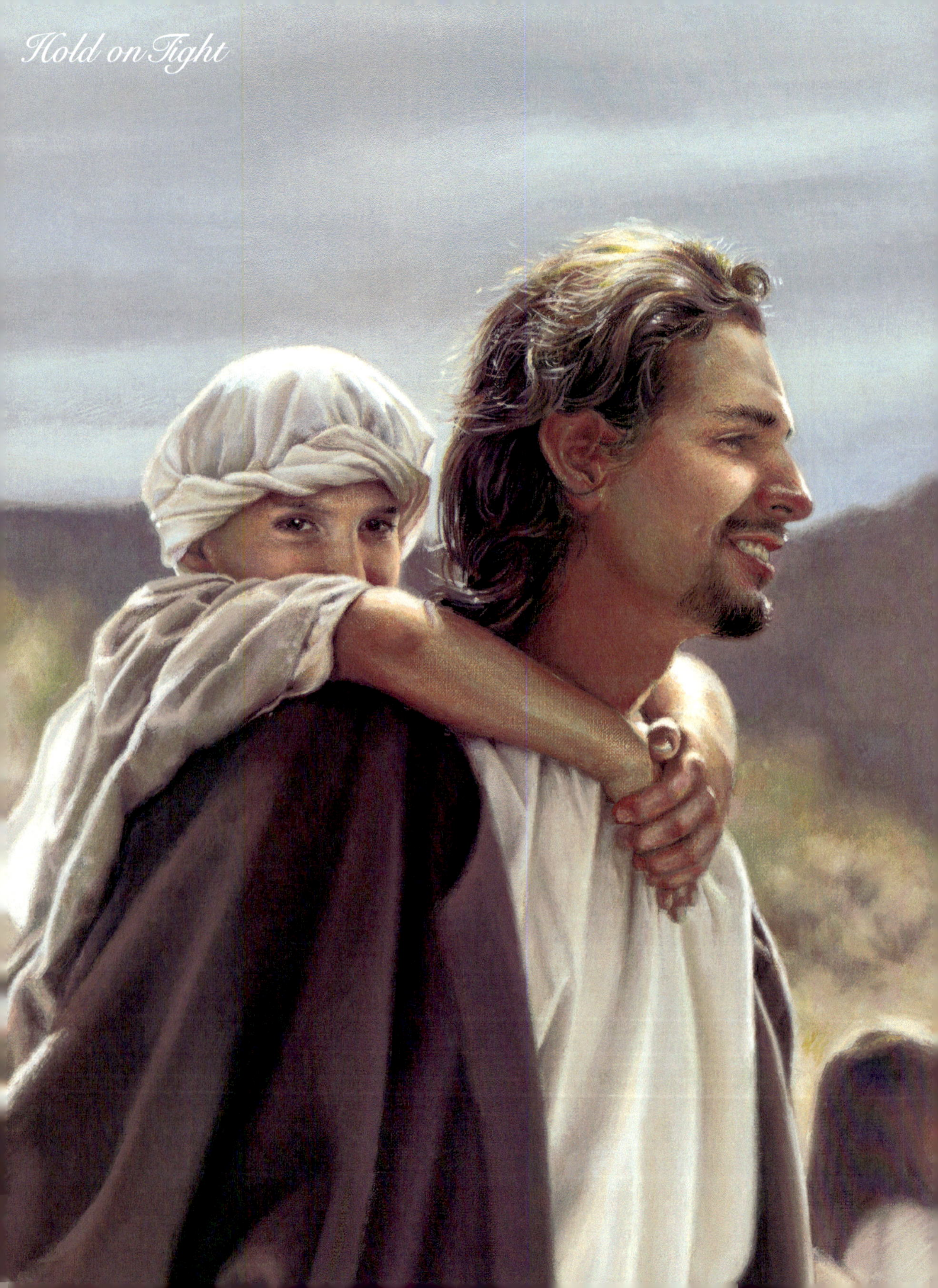
Hold on Tight

He did not bless Phillip feeling that as an Apostle he was unable to bless a model of Christ as it would appear to be an endorsement from the leadership of the Church concerning Christ's appearance. "I will never forget that day," Liz says. "To be in the office of an Apostle with his hands and those of my husband placed upon my head to receive such a glorious blessing—there really aren't words to describe such an experience." He told me that doors would be opened to me through my work that couldn't be opened by the leaders of the Church.

Liz then began "The Son of Man" project, first painting "Hold on Tight" and "Lamb of God," which didn't do as well as the nativity paintings.

This was a learning curve for both Liz and Scott. They learned customers will buy paintings about the nativity, but not so much of paintings depicting other phases in the life of Christ.

Hoping they were wrong, Scott pitched Liz's religious art to the twelve-man board of Hallmark hoping to sign with their religious subsidiary, DaySpring. Hallmark loved Liz's work and was prepared to sign her until they discovered she was a Mormon. They halted the meeting immediately and withdrew their offer to do business. Remembering her blessing from Elder Maxwell, Liz had faith that other doors would be opened to her. At this point Scott didn't know where to pitch Liz's art. Nevertheless, he sent Liz to art galleries throughout the country where few, if any, Latter-day Saints patronized. "At the art galleries there was often a long awkward pause when prospective customers questioned my religion and walked away," Liz says. "There were even a number of art dealers who refused to carry my paintings because I was a 'card-carrying Mormon.'"

Interfaith Success

There were two experiences in Wichita, Kansas, that kept Liz going. At the request of one Greenwich Workshop store, she set up a booth in the back of a Catholic recreation hall to sell her paintings and the book *Son of Man: The Early Years*. In the fair-like atmosphere with lots of children and noise—a throwback to the Relief Society bazaars—shoppers bought crocheted pot holders, candles, cookbooks, and prints of Mary and the baby Jesus. The prints and book were a success with the Catholics, who spoke of Liz's realistic portrayal not found in paintings of Mary done in earlier centuries.

After Liz shut down the booth, she was driven to an art gallery where Catholic women were waiting to speak to her. "One woman looked like she was ready for a fight," Liz says. "I was terrified."

With hands on her hips the woman asked, "Why did you paint Jesus with blue eyes, when everyone knows that Joseph and Mary, being of the House of David, had brown eyes?"

In this setting Liz didn't want to talk about Alexander Neibaur's account of Joseph Smith's First Vision, stating that Jesus had blue eyes. "My immediate thought was I'll be tarred and feathered if I don't come up with a good answer," Liz recalls. "Then I said, 'We only know half of the parentage of Jesus. Joseph wasn't his father.' The woman thought for a moment before saying, 'I never thought of that. You're right.'"

Although a verbal fight had been averted, Liz felt like she had been run through the ringer before another woman approached and asked, "Are you Liz Lemon Swindle?" Liz nodded her head. The woman then asked, "But are you the Mormon Liz Lemon Swindle?" When Liz assured her that she had found the right person, the woman told Liz of flying from South Carolina and having a layover at the Wichita Airport. At the airport she saw an advertisement for the book signing. "I left the airport to tell you something," she said. "You have no idea how affected people are by your art. You'll never know how many lives you have touched." With tears in her eyes, the woman said, "I've got to go and catch my plane." With that, the woman left.

In her next meeting with Elder Maxwell, Liz shared stories of her experience in Wichita and the fact that paintings of Christ other than the nativity were not viable in the current religious art market. She also expressed a recognition that the arts in general were on a downward trajectory and that further paintings in her series on Christ may be hampered or not forthcoming. As she was speaking, Liz reminded herself of the blessing that Elder Maxwell had given her, promising that she would finish this important work on Christ.

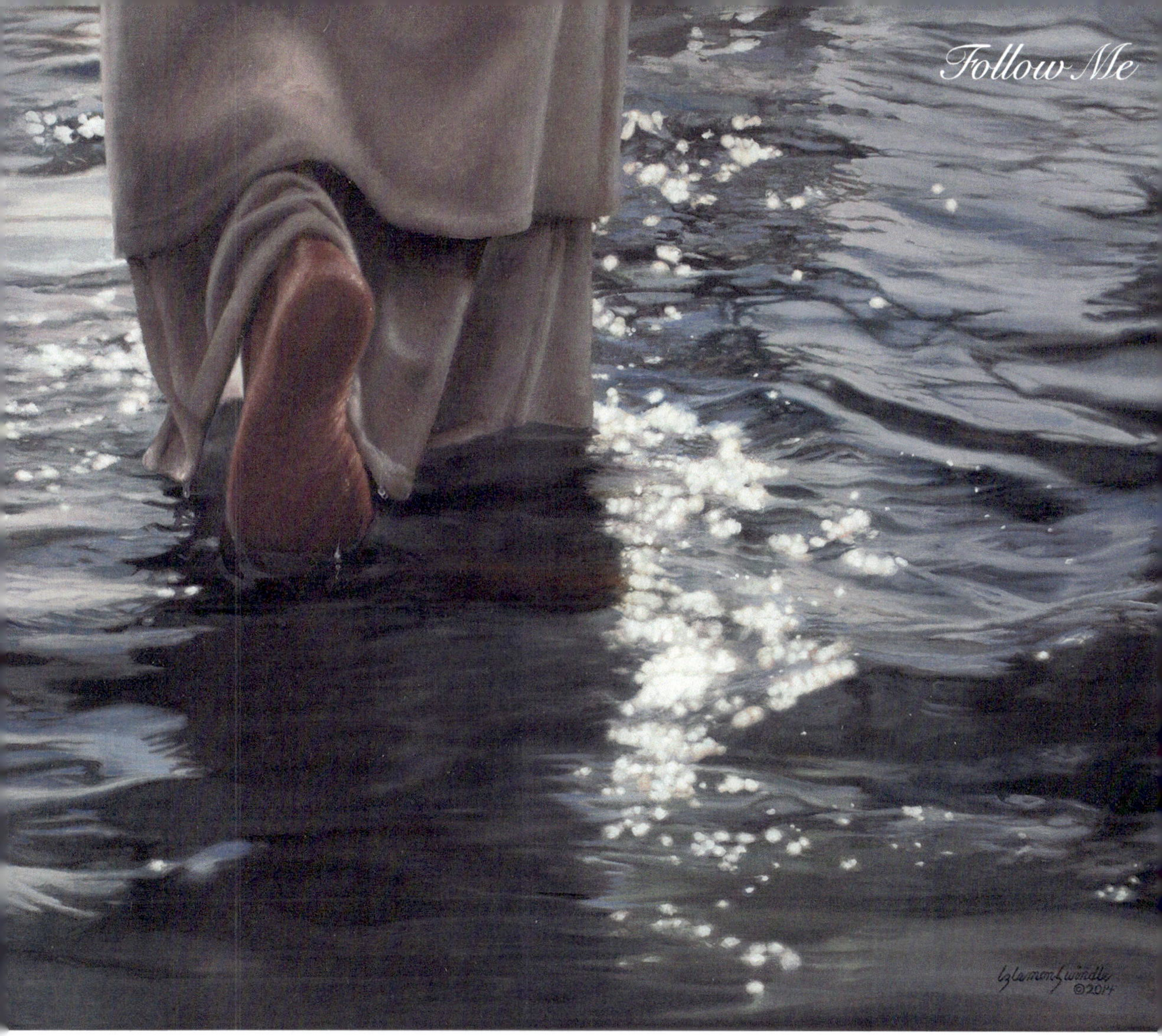

Perhaps being in his presence that day brought the words of the blessing to her memory. The words of the blessing played over and over in her mind on the ride home from Salt Lake.

Finding Christ

In order to succeed, Liz knew it was very important to select the right model to portray a thirty-year-old Christ. Much fasting and prayer went into Liz's choice, for she wanted the model to have the humility and sweetness of Cliff Cole and a powerful countenance that resonated with images of the Savior of the World. Various men approached Liz, including acclaimed actors, saying, "I understand you're looking for a Christ model" and offered their service. *This is exactly why I won't choose you*, Liz thought to herself.

Christopher Croft, a shoe-string relative and student at the University of Utah, caught Liz's attention at a family gathering. He didn't look middle-eastern, and with a short missionary haircut, he didn't look like an ideal model for Christ. Yet Christopher had a powerful, kind countenance. Looking through family albums confirmed Liz's feelings about his looks. She telephoned Christopher and invited him to be her Savior model. "Christopher was more than hesitant," Liz recalls. Yet Liz telephoned Kenneth Cope and left the following message on his answering machine, "I have found the Christ."

Christopher didn't really know what he was getting into except he had six months to grow out his hair before the first photo shoot. The photo shoot took place at an indoor swimming pool in the Kyle and Brenda Powell home. Kenneth, Susan, Jim, and a couple of assistants came to watch as Christopher, dressed in a biblical costume, stood on Plexiglas that rested on two sawhorses in the swimming pool. The photographer asked, "Does Christopher look like he's walking on water?" What he looked like

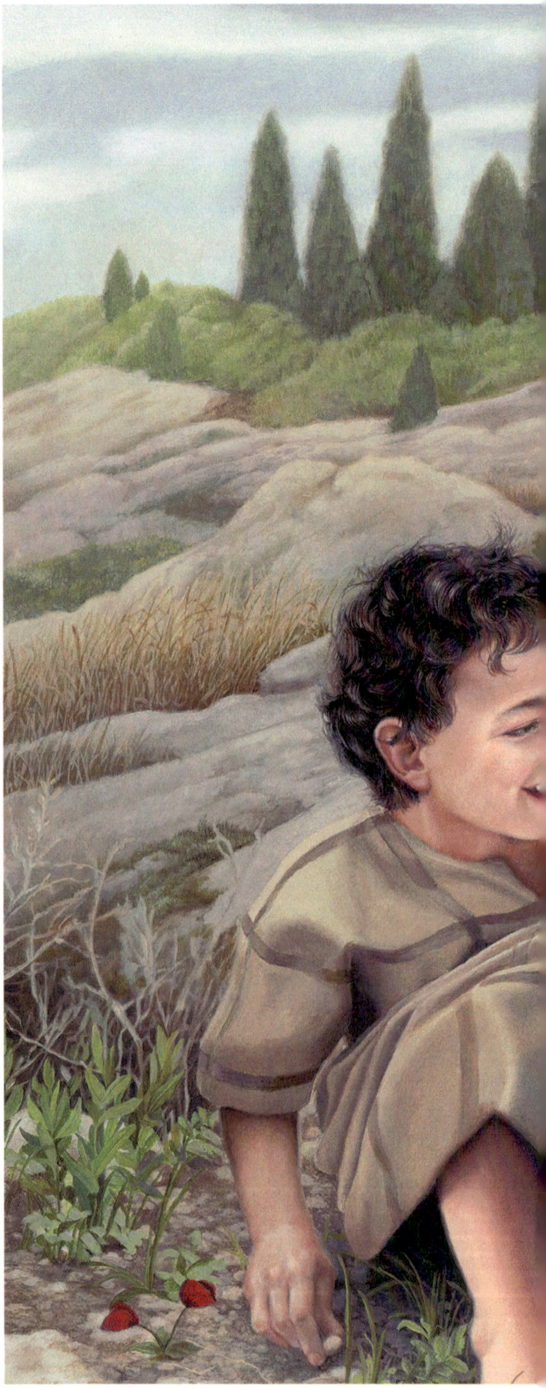

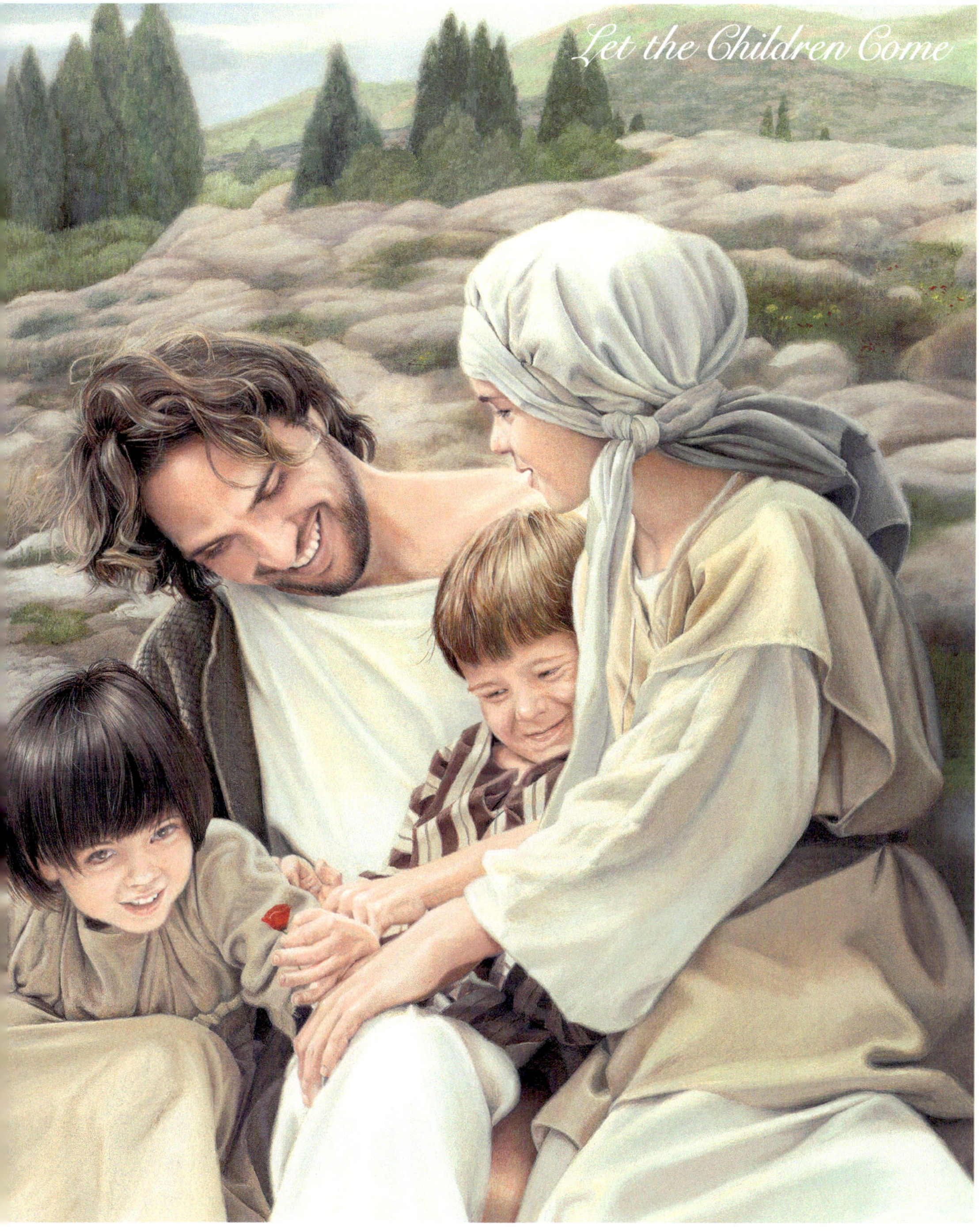
Let the Children Come

to Liz was very uncomfortable. Christopher never liked being the center of attention, but when you stand on Plexiglas in a swimming pool, what else can you be? After the photo shoot Christopher said to Liz, "We need to talk." Liz knew that Christopher wanted out.

Liz concluded that she needed to plan a photo shoot, sooner rather than later, that would be more pleasant for Christopher than walking on Plexiglas in water. Knowing something of his love of children, Liz put together a photo shoot where he would interact with children. The day of the photo shoot was windy and foreboding. The skies threatened with rain and lightning. Between downpours the photographer captured much-needed material for upcoming paintings. The children were dressed in biblical attire and stood at the bottom of a small hill as the photographer, camera in hand, stood at the top. On the other side of the hill was Christopher dressed as Christ with Bucky and Jerry Swiss dressed as Christ's apostles. The plan was to bring both parties to the summit and capture on film the exact moment when the children recognized Jesus. The plan went off without a hitch. "It's Jesus!" the children shouted. They ran to him, threw their arms around him, and squealed with delight. "Christopher's sparkling blue eyes seemed to dance," Liz says. "I felt relieved."

But that night Christopher telephoned Liz and said, "I'm on my way to your house." Just before he arrived, the mother of one of the young children who yelled, "Jesus!" knocked on the door, handed Liz a letter, and quickly left. Liz read, "We adopted our son when he was a newborn and I've never been able to bond with him. When I saw him run to Jesus and watched as he was scooped up in those loving arms, I was overwhelmed with the idea of the Savior loving my son, so I resolved to work harder to create a bond with my son." When Christopher arrived at the house a few minutes later, Liz handed him the letter to read. "If anything was going to touch Christopher's heart it was the feelings of this mother about her son," Liz says. "It's not only the Lord sending angels when needed; it's His perfect timing too."

"Christopher stayed in the project for five years," Liz recalls. "He was the perfect Christ model." It wasn't until after he finished that Liz realized just what she had asked of him. Liz assumed Christopher would be flattered to portray Christ and not have any reservations. But portraying the Savior of the World isn't that simple. Christopher was asked to step for a moment into the shoes of the only perfect man who has ever lived on the earth and convey the feelings that one would assume Christ had. His hesitation to portray Jesus Christ had everything to do with his feelings of being unequal to the task. "To ask a very shy young man to act out those feelings before a film crew and strangers is beyond anything an artist has a right to ask," Liz says. "To put things in perspective, Christopher's temple wedding photos show him with longer hair than his bride. I can't think of anyone that would agree to such a request, except Christopher and maybe his replacement, Phillip."

Painting the Holy Land

Liz has often spoken of one challenge faced in the "Son of Man" project that included Christopher and his new bride—a planned trip to Israel. Before anyone stepped on the plane, Liz had costumes made for Christopher, ordered a generator to be taken up to the Mount of Olives, hired Palestinians to move equipment, and rented studio lights from the only television station in the country. Liz; her photographer; Kenneth Cope; her book designer, Scott Eggers; her model for Mary Magdalene, Paqui Handy; the model's husband, Dan Handy; Kathy Swiss; and Sue Mason caught a morning flight at the Salt Lake Airport and headed to Jerusalem. Christopher and his wife were to catch the afternoon flight.

After being delayed in France for nine hours and an unexpected flight to Sweden, Liz and her party arrived in Jerusalem. Before checking into her room, Liz asked the hotel concierge if Christopher Croft had already checked in. The answer was, "No." When the answer was still "no" a few hours later Liz telephoned Bucky in Utah to ask him about the whereabouts of Christopher. After a day of trying to contact Christopher, Bucky said, "It's a long story but Christopher and his wife decided to not go to Israel. Christopher tried twice to board the plane with his wife, Suzanne, but the Spirit held him back. He knew you would be frantic with worry, but he just felt like he wasn't supposed to be there."

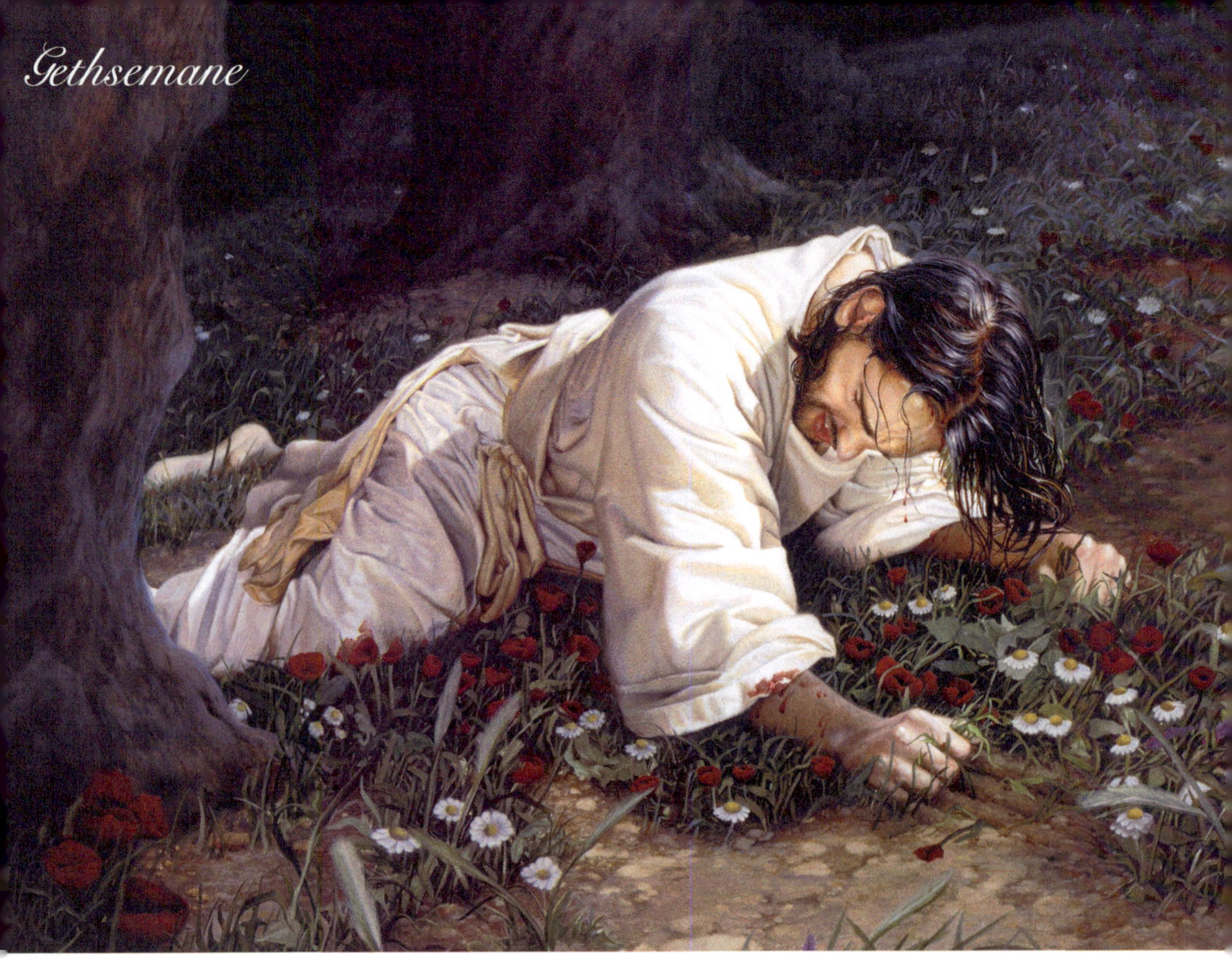

Liz was beyond frantic by this point, but Bucky reassured her that things were as they should be and she needed to proceed. That was the beginning of what proved a very difficult three weeks for Liz. Her photographer could film scenery and background filler, but without Christopher at the Mount of Beatitudes, the Sea of Galilee, or in the Upper Room, the trip seemed pointless. A lost passport, a union revolt, and gouging prices to rent a boat at night on the Sea of Galilee were the norm for the trip. Liz kept hoping that things would get better, but instead they grew worse each day.

"I tried to improvise with another model," Liz says. "I couldn't use the model's face but I could use his body for such scenes as the agony of Gethsemane." In Gethsemane, Liz had Dan Handy lean against a tree. Liz thought she would paint the Gethsemane scene like other artists had portrayed the Atonement.

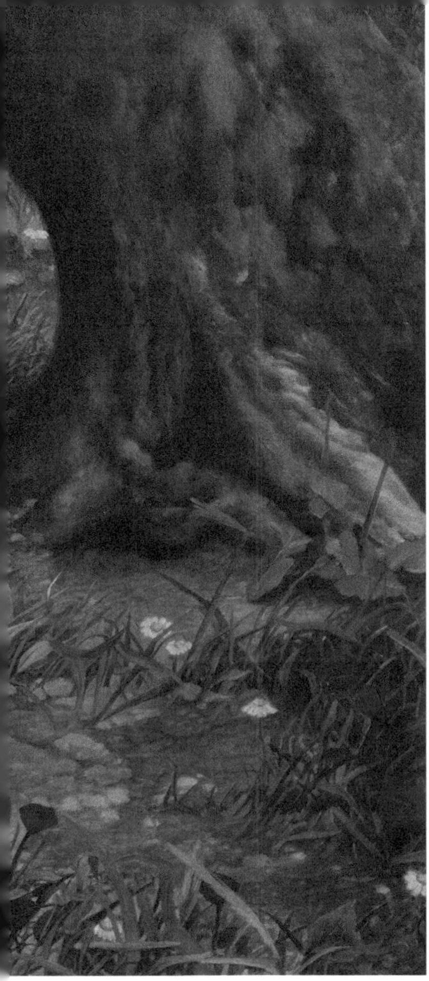

"I think the Savior would be on His knees and fall to the ground," Kenneth said. Liz reluctantly agreed and had the model kneel down and then fall to the ground in agony. When he stood up, his robes were stained red from poppies growing on the ground beneath him.

On their last day at the Garden Tomb, Kenneth said with anticipation, "This is going to be good."

Liz says, "I nearly choked him. All I wanted to do was go home. I thought the trip a waste of time and a waste of 32,000 dollars—an expensive price tag for weeks of disappointment." It was not until Liz's photographer handed her photographs from the trip that Liz saw the hand of the Lord in her travels. Rays of sunlight and picturesque scenes gave her a reference point for future paintings. Only then did she feel gratitude for the privilege of being in the Holy Land.

Hopes, Dreams, and Facts

As Israel moved from the front burner to the back, Liz foresaw "smooth sailing ahead." Her original paintings were selling quickly to avid collectors, and her prints were in high demand. She had a two-year waiting list for paintings and a schedule with imposing deadlines. Frameworks and Repartee Gallery were on solid footing and what had been excessive bills piling up on American Express cards were paid without batting an eyelash. Liz and Bucky had started looking for a new house.

In this prosperous period of their lives, Liz and Bucky received a FedEx envelope containing ten shares of investment stock, a gift from Jerry Moore (name changed). Jerry was a friend, a venture capitalist, and an art collector. Liz had been painting at the Independence Visitors' Center in Missouri and had just returned home for the weekend when the gallery called asking if she had any new works because there was a gentleman there who wanted to purchase an original. "The piece I had brought home with me was still wet," Liz says. "Jerry bought the painting 'Go with Me to Cumorah' for 9,000 dollars that very day."

As the years passed, Jerry and his wife, Shauna, became dear friends with Bucky and Liz. Every fall around Halloween, Liz and Bucky would visit them in Las Vegas. The annual trip usually included a fireside and sometimes a private home show.

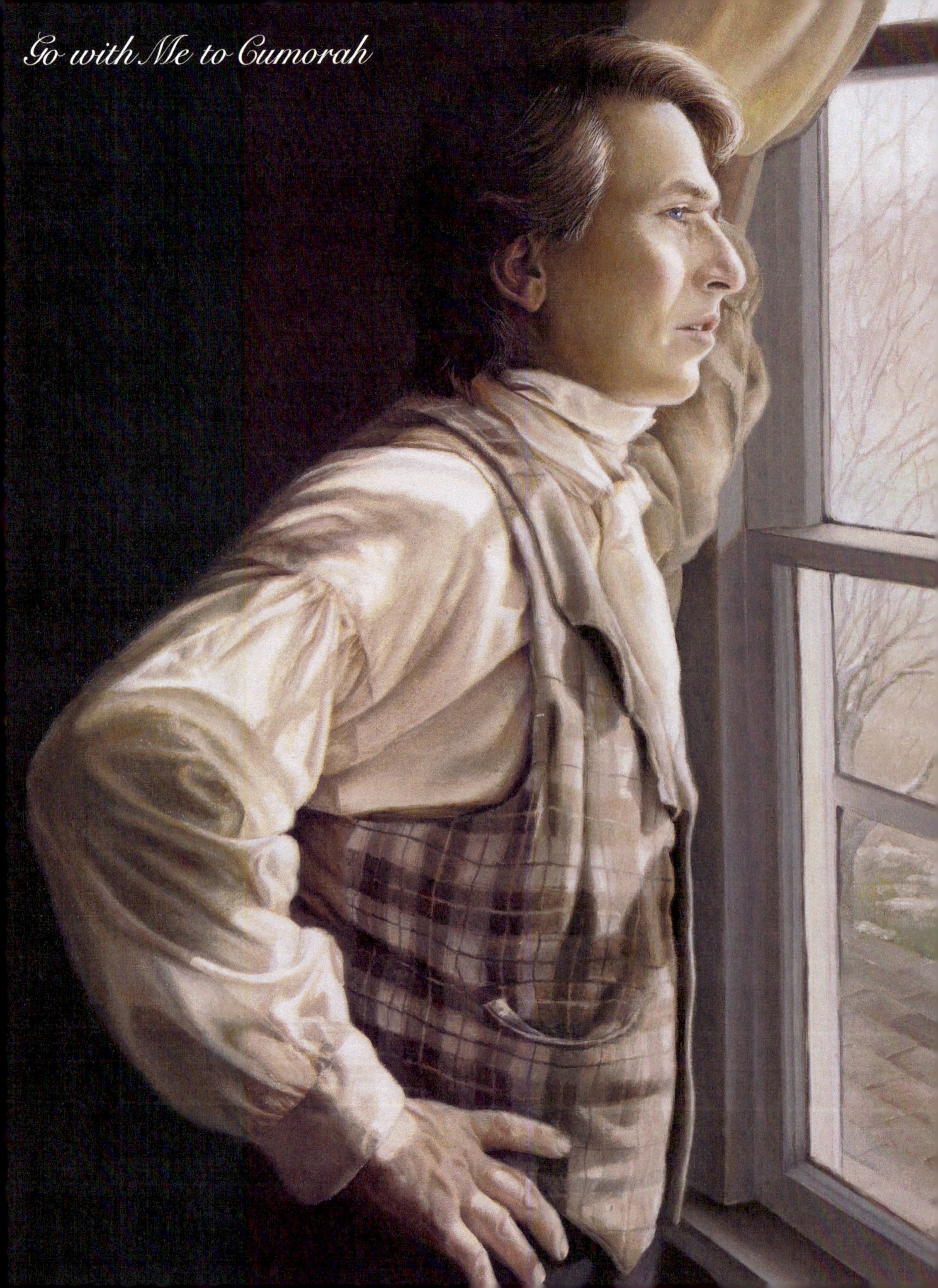

Go with Me to Cumorah

Liz recalls her first visit to the Moore's home: "I was picked up at the Las Vegas airport and driven to their home. On the drive we passed beautiful, expansive mansions. With righteous indignation, I said to Shauna, 'How can people justify living in such a house when there are so many people starving in the world? It doesn't seem right.'" Shauna kept driving and didn't say anything about Liz's comment. She pulled the car in the driveway of a very nice and spacious 6,000-square-foot home. Cars and boats made for a tight fit in the driveway. While seated in the kitchen, I was shown floor plans for a 32,000-square-foot home," Liz says. "I was shown photographs of a chandelier that had arrived that day from Europe for the Moore's new home."

Millionaires

Liz didn't know much about stocks and assumed that each of the ten shares was worth ten dollars and Jerry had given her a hundred dollars. She had no idea that he was restructuring his estate and redistributing his funds. She called Jerry to thank him for the gift and ask what was going on. Jerry's wife answered, "In a year from now, you'll either love or hate us."

Liz said, "That's weird. Do you want to explain?"

"Next time you come to Vegas, we'll explain everything," she said.

On their next trip to Vegas, Liz and Bucky sat with the Moores around a large table in their exquisite mansion. Jerry took the occasion to explain that he was the broker on a banking deal that would net him a dividend of 1.2 billion dollars. He pointed to a magazine article featuring Donald Trump and said, "This year I'll make more money than that guy, and I'll use my money for good." After Jerry had talked for about twenty minutes, he asked Liz, "Aren't you the least bit curious how much ten shares are worth?" Before Liz could answer, Jerry said, "Your shares are worth 9.2 million dollars." Bucky nearly slid off his chair. Liz asked him to tell her again and wanted to know how this was possible. Liz wanted to know what the catch was and what he wanted them to do with the money. "Whatever you want," Jerry said. "It's your money."

Liz's first thought was, "I'm going to order all my paint brushes for five years, instead of my usual order." She then thought of how she had tried to paint for altruistic purposes alone and not for money; now she could. Next came the thought that worries over not having enough paint to finish a painting and the cost of a large canvas were no longer issues. Liz figured that in interest alone, their shares would soon be worth 12 million dollars. Bucky was more skeptical and had the presence of mind to think, *Let's not count our chickens before they hatch.*

When Bucky and Liz returned to Utah, their accountant looked over the paperwork that Jerry had given them and said, "Everything comes up roses. You are about to be one of the wealthiest couples in Orem." Liz partied with her children and friends. Although swamped with work, she didn't care. Deadlines slipped as she contemplated what she would do with so much money and trusted in a world she knew nothing about. Bucky, on the other hand, maintained the voice of reason. He told Liz, "Calm down. Until the money is in the bank, let's not get too excited. Let's not forget our good friend Murphy" (meaning Murphy's Law). One thing was for sure—9 million dollars would change their lives.

Liz's Dream Fulfilled

Time passed slowly. There were reports that Jerry was heading to Germany to seal the deal and that a check would come their way soon. This was followed by reports of needing to postpone and reschedule meetings with J. P. Morgan. Occasionally Jerry telephoned. "I thought that I would be giving you a check by now, but we're still negotiating," he'd say. "Cross your fingers that I'll come home from Europe with a check."

Liz put her life on hold waiting for the next phone call from Jerry until she had a dream. In her dream she walked into a beautiful circular room that had a large dresser with a jeweled treasure chest on top. As Liz reached for the chest and pulled it down close to her, she noticed some of the jewels were missing. She opened up the chest and found it full of gold coins, rubies, and diamonds. She could feel the coins in her hands and hear them clank together in the chest. Then she felt her mother standing near her. Her mother was dressed in white and looked noble, if not royal. "Now is not the time," her mother said. Liz closed the treasure chest, put it back on top of the dresser, and awakened.

Shortly after the dream, J. P. Morgan and small banks across the nation and around the world crashed. Frameworks and Repartee Galleries teetered under what had become a nationwide economic downturn. It was almost impossible to make a decent living selling art when banks had crashed, the mortgage industry collapsed, and families were losing their homes. Artists were frustrated that their works weren't selling at the galleries. They put down their brushes and took full-time jobs in other fields to feed their families. There was little that could be done with brick and mortar galleries except shut the door or ride out the recession.

Repartee in Crisis

The issue Bucky faced was there were three types of customers who patronized the Repartee Galleries. One type was high-end buyers who were looking for original art to put on the walls of their mansions. These customers made up about one percent of Repartee customers. With the economic downturn, the high-end buyers feared a recession and held on to their money instead of covering their walls with art. The second type of patrons were customers in the middle income bracket—married couples living in their second home. They bought large prints for their walls, but not original paintings. The middle market was wiped out in the crash. The third type were customers in the lower income group who bought matte 5"×7" prints. They were students or those on a tighter budget. They continued to patronize the galleries. Repartee Galleries could not be sustained by those on tight budgets. The crisis was real.

At this critical juncture, Liz's son Steevun asked Bucky, "How would you feel if I worked for you?" Steevun was employed with Mainstream Satellite, a company that sold to larger companies like NBC. He was cautious in business and was on the fast track in the satellite company. He had a large cherrywood desk and original paintings on the walls of his 20'×20' office located in the research park of east Salt Lake. It appeared to Liz and to Steevun's employer that Steevun was succeeding. Liz learned one morning that Steevun had quit his job and was working for Repartee Galleries when she saw him at the warehouse. "What are you doing here?" she asked. Steevun replied, "I'm looking for a door for my office. It's my first day. I'm working here now. I'm the general manager responsible for day-to-day operations."

As manager, Steevun began to downsize right away. He closed a gallery in Bountiful and one in the Salt Lake mall. He renegotiated contracts and started printing calendars for the lower end market. When Steevun realized that Greenwich Workshops was selling to customers that Bucky had built up and leaving Repartee out of the transactions, he began negotiating to get Liz out of her contract with Greenwich. Although Greenwich was resistant and Scott Usher was well aware that the first book he published in the "Son of Man" series on the nativity sold like hotcakes, he was just as aware that the second book on the miracles of Jesus sold only partially as well and the last book on the crucifixion bombed. "At Easter, buyers would rather purchase worthless stuffed bunnies than a book on the crucifixion and resurrection of Christ," Liz says. Using the book issue as leverage and the fact that Repartee needed full rights to Liz's work to survive in the down economy, an amicable solution was reached.

Seeing the Blessings

Without Greenwich backing her work, Liz found it difficult to continue in a national market. Although publicity personnel were hired, they ran up against bias due largely to her LDS faith. The roadblocks did not stop Liz from continuing to paint the life of the Savior and pray that opportunities would present themselves. In her field, there's always a chance great things will happen, but just as big a chance that nothing will come of it. One great opportunity came when a Catholic employee received an email from Archbishop Denoya one Friday night requesting a license to create a personal Christmas card using Liz's painting "Be It unto Me." The employee relayed the message to Steevun the following Monday. Steevun put it aside, saying he'd get to it later, but the Catholic employee told him that Repartee Galleries needed to handle the inquiry more personally as an archbishop in the Catholic Church is similar to a member of the Seventy in the LDS Church. He told Steevun that such a request was a great compliment and a door to future interactions. Following his advice, Steevun called Archbishop Denoya, agreeing to the license for the card and, per request, promising to send two prints of the painting—one for the Pope as a Christmas gift from the archbishop and one for the archbishop himself

Months later, the archbishop sent a copy of the card that he had licensed and a note of thanks. When Steevun called to thank him for the card, Archbishop

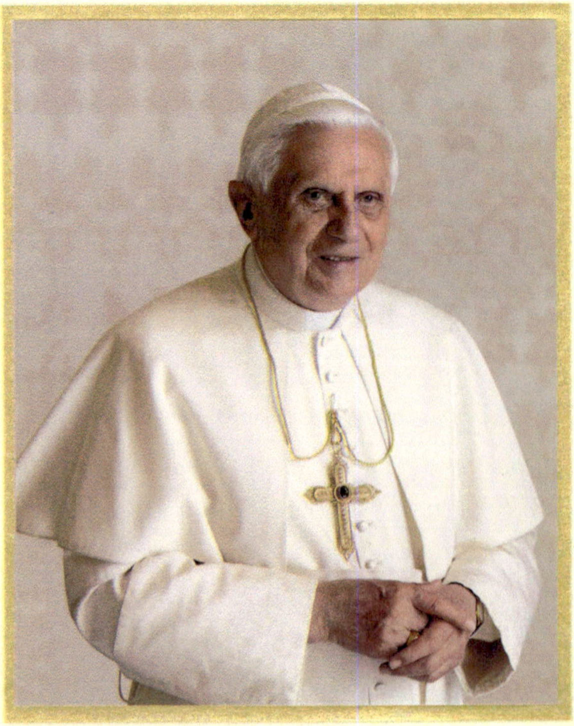

His Holiness Benedict XVI

cordially imparts the requested

Apostolic Blessing to

Liz Lemon Swindle

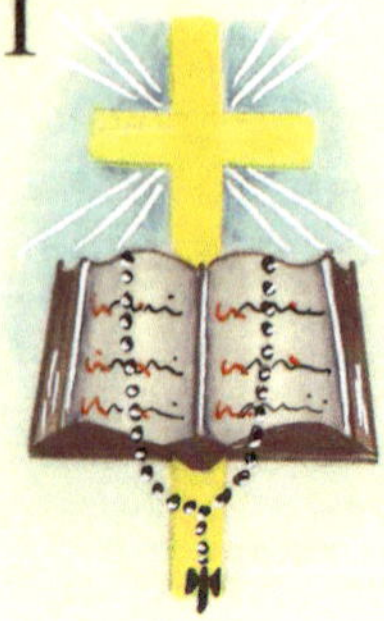

for her life of deep faith bringing faith to life
through her service and through her art
invoking an abundance of divine graces

Ex Aedibus Vaticanis, die 6.10.2010

+ Félix del Blanco Prieto

Archiepiscopus Eleemosynarius Apostolicus

Denoya said, "The Pope loved the painting 'Be It unto Me.' He has hung the painting in his private living quarters." Later Liz received a picture of Pope Benedict and a handwritten note in gold calligraphy. The note was a papal blessing. When Liz asked the Catholic coworker what it meant, he said, "God would have to give you a blessing to get one better than this. This is an honored gift of love from our beloved Pope."

Painting the Parables

Although Liz had once again extended herself to an ever-widening audience, as evidenced by the papal blessing, she felt discomforted that she had focused on painting the life of Christ and not on the Savior's teachings. She had painted the visit of the wise men, the suffering in Gethsemane, and the Last Supper, but where were her paintings of charity, loving your neighbor, and forgiveness? For that matter, where were her paintings of the parables? With a painting schedule as long as her arm and demands on her time that seemed impossible to keep, Liz started painting the Master's teachings. Knowing that she could not create large mural-like paintings with her other commitments, she began to create small paintings of the parables. (The size of the painting matters. The bigger it is the more time it takes. Small paintings go fast.)

With creating small paintings came a renewed excitement to Liz's work. Sharing in her excitement was investor and philanthropist James Clark. He wanted to buy each of her paintings on the parables. When Liz cautiously suggested that there could be as many as twelve, James said, "You'll know when they're done." As Liz completed the first of what became dozens of parables, she showed her work to potential buyers expecting that they would rejoice with her in the painting. Instead they said, "Oh, that's nice."

"They didn't grasp the idea that the painting of the parable had application to themselves," Liz says. "This seemed odd to me, for these same people were trying to hang on to their sanity and get through life. They couldn't see that the parable related to them."

Liz asked Bucky, "How can I get people to understand that there is more to the painting of a parable than 'that's nice'?"

Bucky said, "You need to make it apply to their everyday lives. Paint our day—paint modern and biblical." When Liz put her first modern interpretation of a parable next to the biblical painting, people got it.

"I see it," they said. "The parable relates to me."

"It was as if the modern painting gave them CliffsNotes to the Savior's parable," Liz says. Her paintings of the parables were shown to executives at the Springville Art Museum. They were so approving of her artist renderings that the museum featured Liz's work in a yearlong show even though not all of her parables had a modern counterpart.

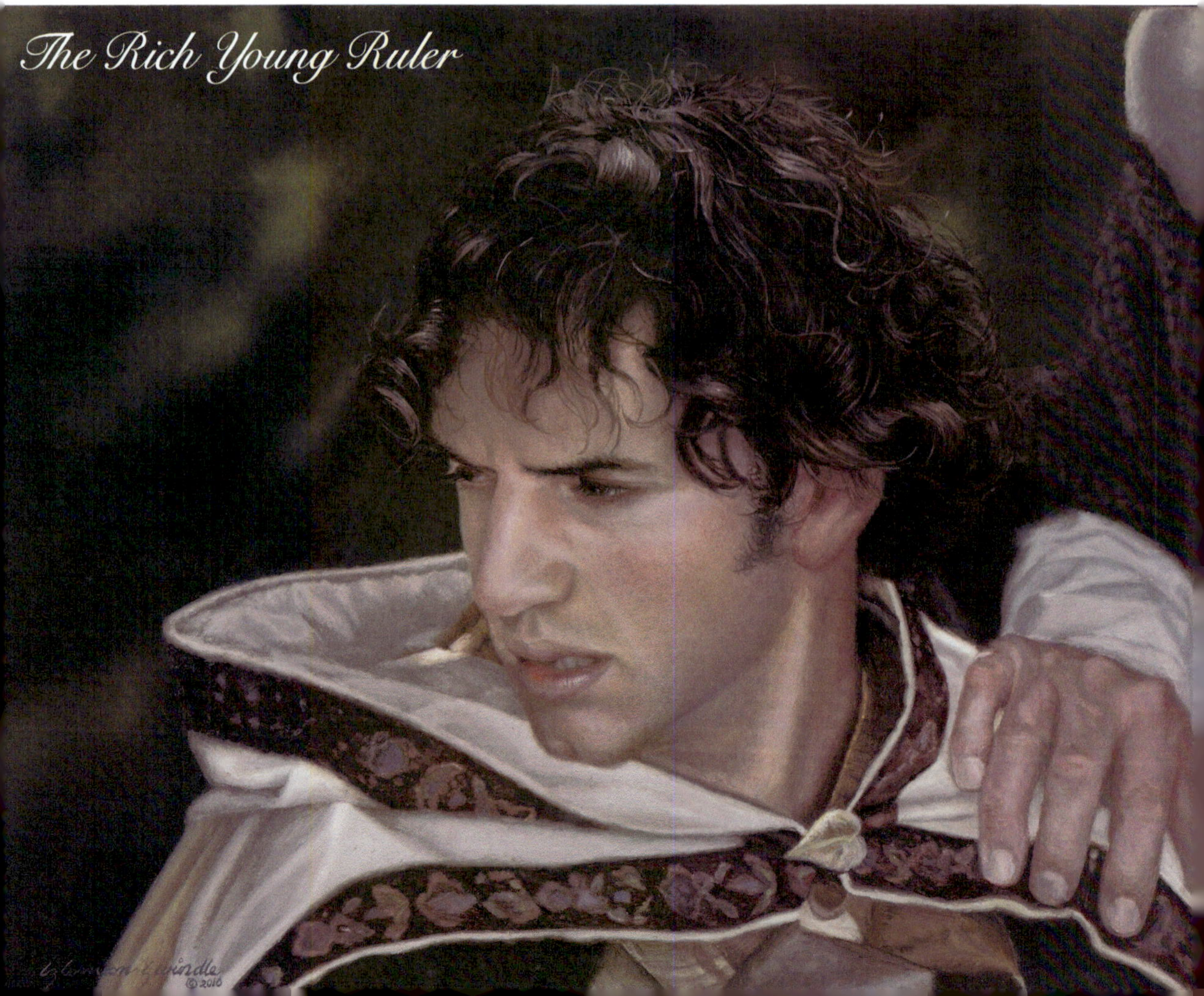

The Rich Young Ruler

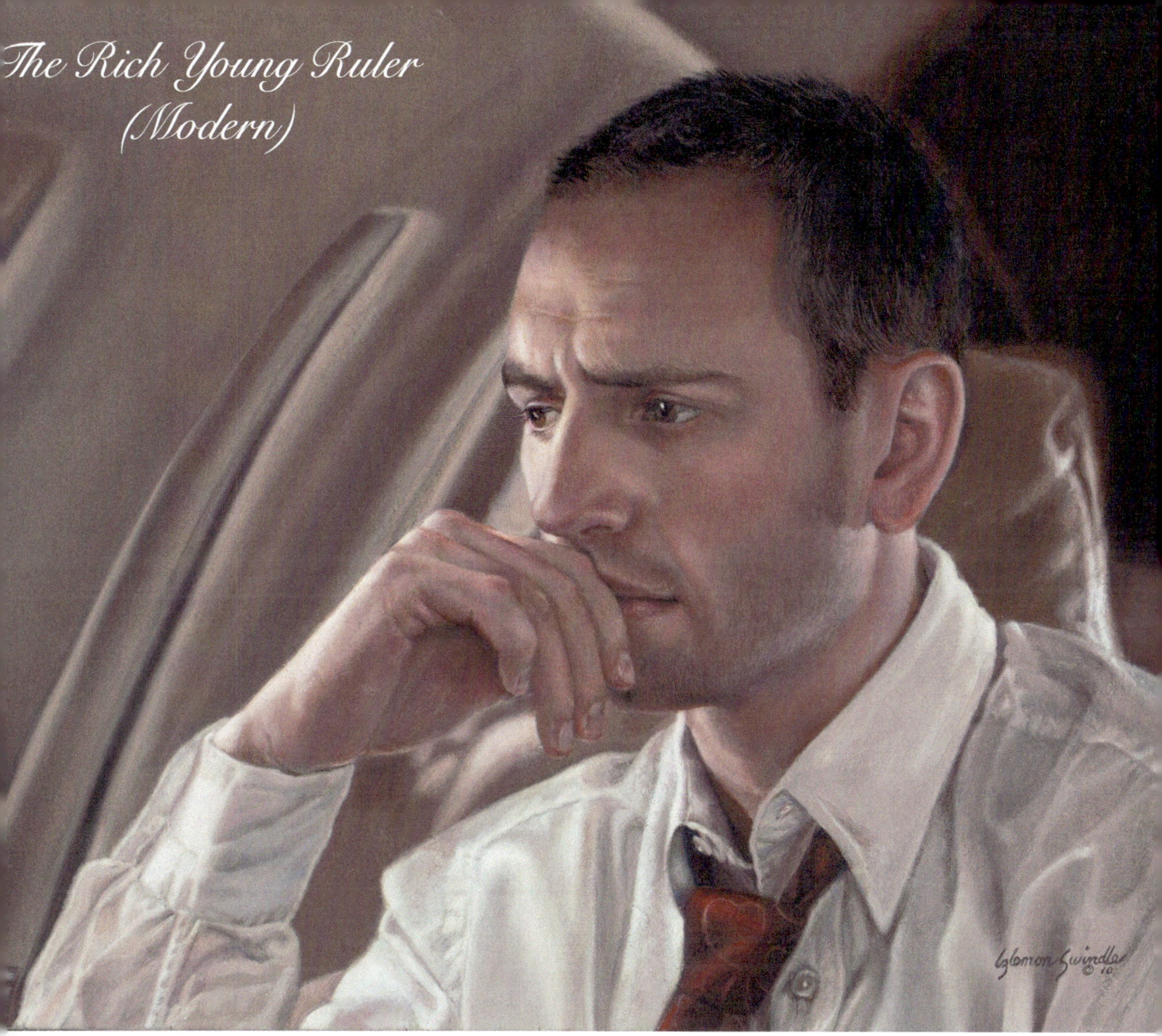

TETHERED TO THE LORD

As crowds lined up in the museum to see her latest work, Liz accepted a commission to paint twelve mural-like paintings (64"×80") on the New Testament. To cover such large surfaces required by the commission was not easy. As a detailed artist, who insists on painting every individual blade of grass or cloud in the sky, such repetitive motion of the paintbrush in hand day after day took its toll. Feeling her right hand cramping more than usual, Liz sought medical advice. She was diagnosed with rheumatoid arthritis. At a crossroads, Liz needed to decide whether to continue painting or throw in the towel.

One day while meeting with long-time friend Henry B. Eyring, President Eyring mentioned some bad new he had received and that while he felt

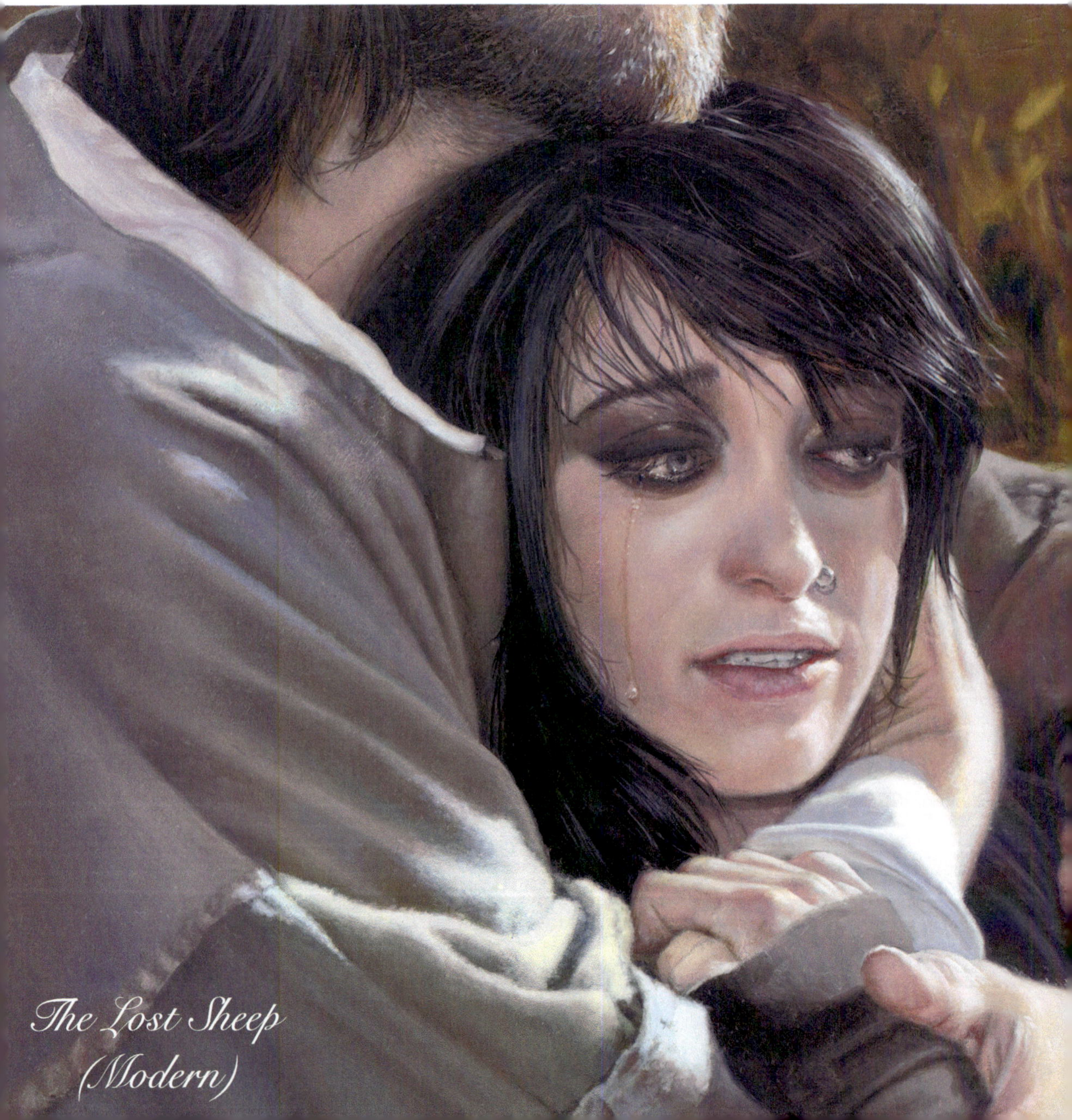

The Lost Sheep (Modern)

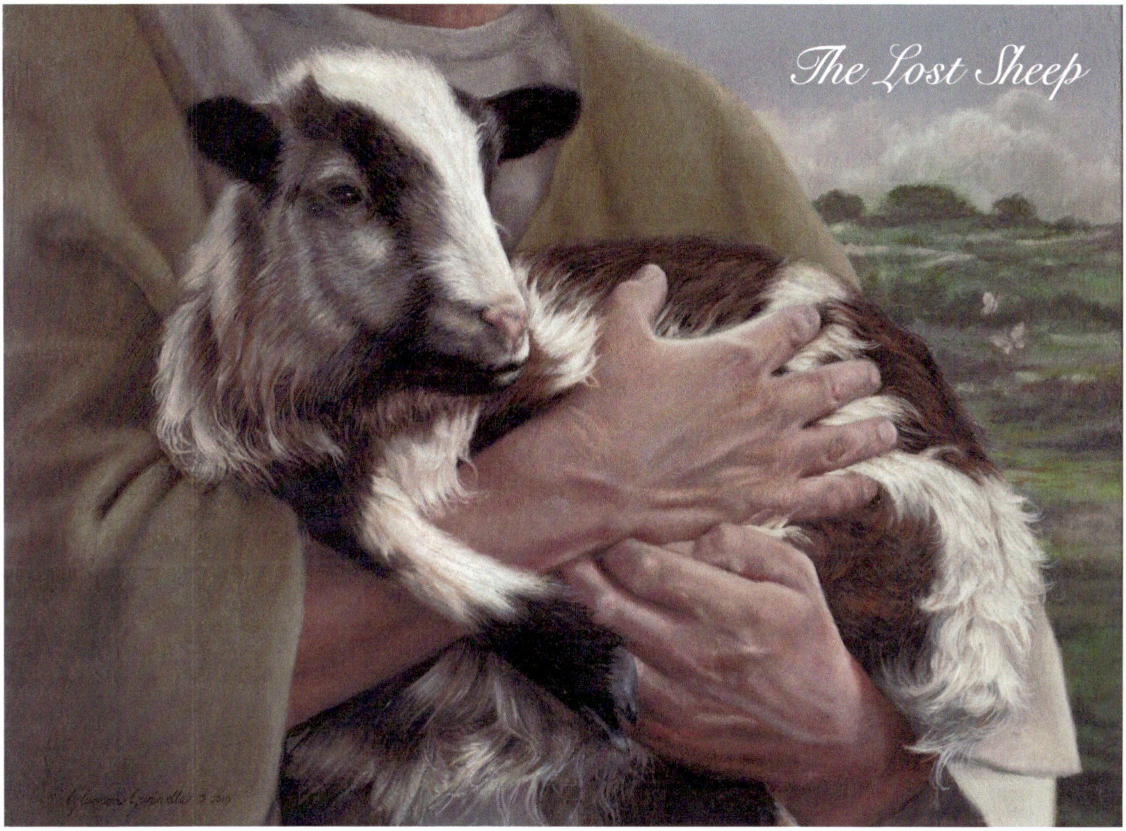

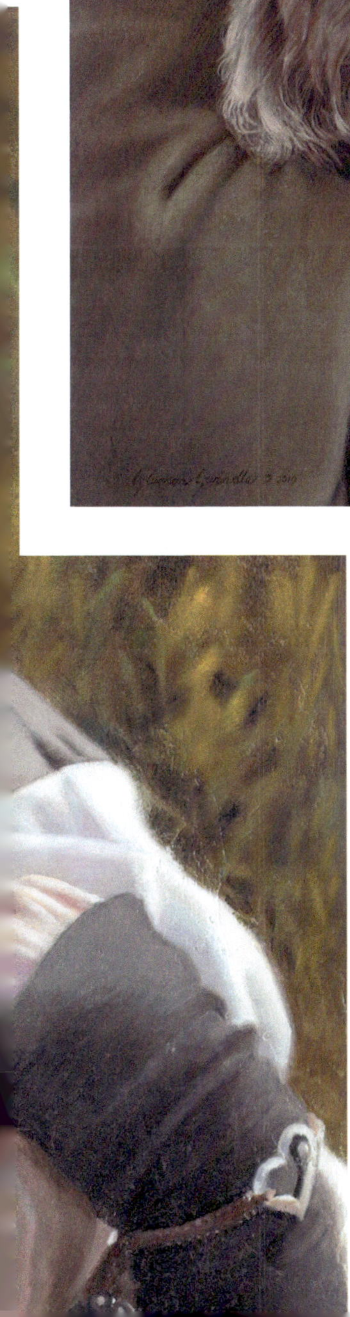

burdened, he also felt comforted knowing that this experience would bring him closer to the Lord. Hearing that, Liz shared her recent news of being diagnosed with rheumatoid arthritis and the struggle it had been thus far. President Eyring said, "Isn't that wonderful that Heavenly Father has found a way to keep you tethered to Him." His comment was profound and inspired. On difficult days, it is a comfort to Liz to look at her limitations as blessings.

When the arthritis flares up so bad that hand cramps can only be resolved by medical attention, Liz recalls a priesthood blessing given by her bishop: "Heavenly Father is pleased with your work. When you pass through the veil to the other side, the Savior will take you in his arms and thank you. You will be given all of your days. You will be able to finish your work." With renewed courage she picks up her paintbrush and starts anew, for commissioned paintings await the talented artist. There is still much to do and little time to lament, "If only." For the most renowned LDS artist of our time, her reason for continuing to paint is clear—Jesus is the Christ.

Conclusion

Liz is now busier than ever. Demands for her originals are high, and her prints are hard to keep in stock. Steevun's business background has blessed her family and their employees. Bryun, her second son, is realizing his dream of creating games for families. He and his wife are raising eight children. Mishel and her family live in Baltimore where she is a nurse at Johns Hopkins and her husband is an artist and restores historic sites in the nation's capital. Loree and her family live in New Jersey. She enjoys writing and her husband finds satisfaction in being a maxi-facial surgeon. Jenifer and her family live in South Dakota. Jenifer's husband is working on his doctorate and teaching at a university. Liz and Bucky's first grandson left for his mission in July 2016, and another grandson is attending Brigham Young University before leaving on his mission next summer. The other sixteen grandchildren are excelling in sports, music, art, math, and science, but more importantly, according to their grandmother Liz, "They are all great kids who are being raised by great parents."

Liz takes time from her busy schedule to reflect on the priesthood blessing of Elder Maxwell in which she was promised "a happy family where her home would be filled with love and laughter and that she would finish the work she was meant to do." On the shelves of her studio are photographs of Elder Maxwell and President Thomas S. Monson. On her desk sits the papal blessing from Pope Benedict. Strewn around her studio on easels and canvases are artworks in progress depicting the events and teachings of the life of Jesus Christ. The parables—both modern and biblical—finished and unfinished, as well as thousands of scrap from countless photo shoots, sit in files and boxes waiting for the famed artist to pick up her brush and begin. One day, in the not too distant future, the artistic renderings of Liz Lemon Swindle that so readily testify of Jesus being the Savior of the World will find their place in homes of devoted Christians around the world.

Liz Lemon Swindle Gallery with Commentary

While Liz's testimony is evident in her paintings, it is reiterated in her commentary on the paintings included in this gallery.

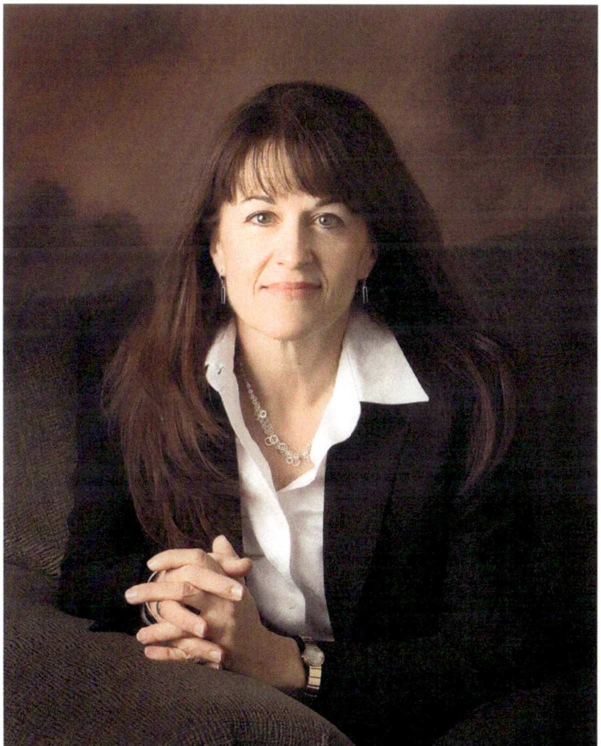

Surely the Savior knew from an early age the path that lay ahead of Him, yet He was not discouraged or dismayed. He went about doing good and filled His life, and the lives of others, with joy and happiness.

I am inspired by the story of Reverend Henry Lyte. Henry's father abandoned the family while he was a young boy and his mother died shortly after. In addition to being orphaned at an early age, Henry struggled throughout his life with poor health—yet all that knew him commented on his cheery temperament. His final contribution came just three weeks before his death. Though he was dying of tuberculosis, Henry was still determined to give to others. He rose from his bed and penned the words that would become the cherished hymn, "Abide with Me."

Certainly none of us can walk through life free from illness and despair, but we each can decide how we will respond to those trials that come. This painting reminds me that when trials come, I can choose to retreat into myself, or reach out as the Savior did and bring happiness to others. Only through selfless sacrifice can we ever hope to abide with the Lord.

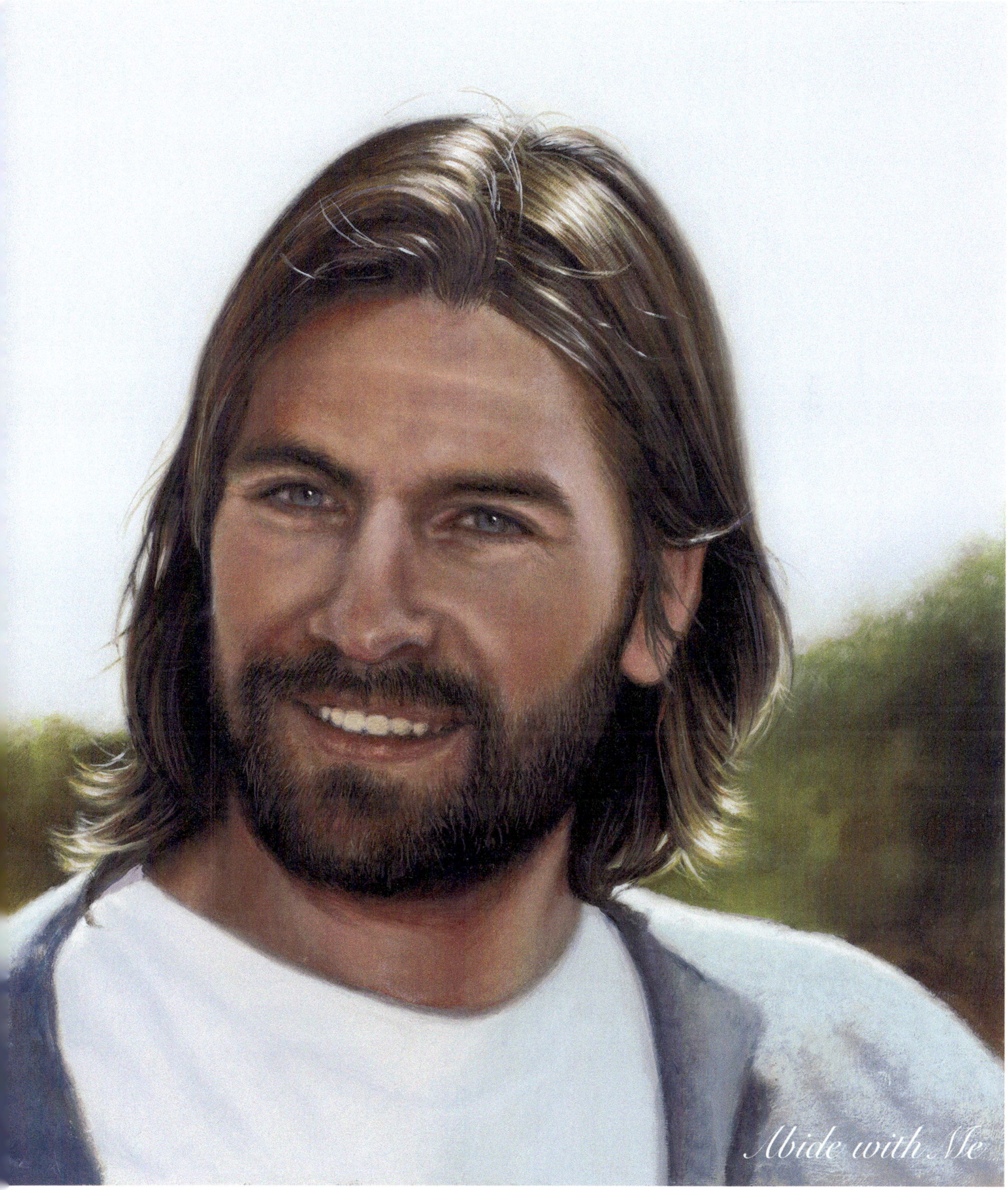
Abide with Me

Two thousand years ago, the Savior stood on the shores of Galilee teaching the crowds. As night fell, He perceived the people were hungry and asked His disciples to gather what food they could. He then took their "five loaves and two fishes" and fed the five thousand.

A few days later, the crowds again returned to the shores of Galilee, but this time the Savior met them saying, "Ye seek me, not because ye saw the miracles, but because ye did eat of the loaves, and were filled . . . from that time many of his disciples went back, and walked no more with him" (John 6:26, 67).

Are we like the crowds who follow the Savior when life is easy and our are bellies full, only to abandon Him when things grow hard? It is my witness that hardship is the cement of discipleship and that only in the midst of our failing health, our wayward children, and tough economic times can we truly understand the peace that comes from heeding His words, "Come Follow Me."

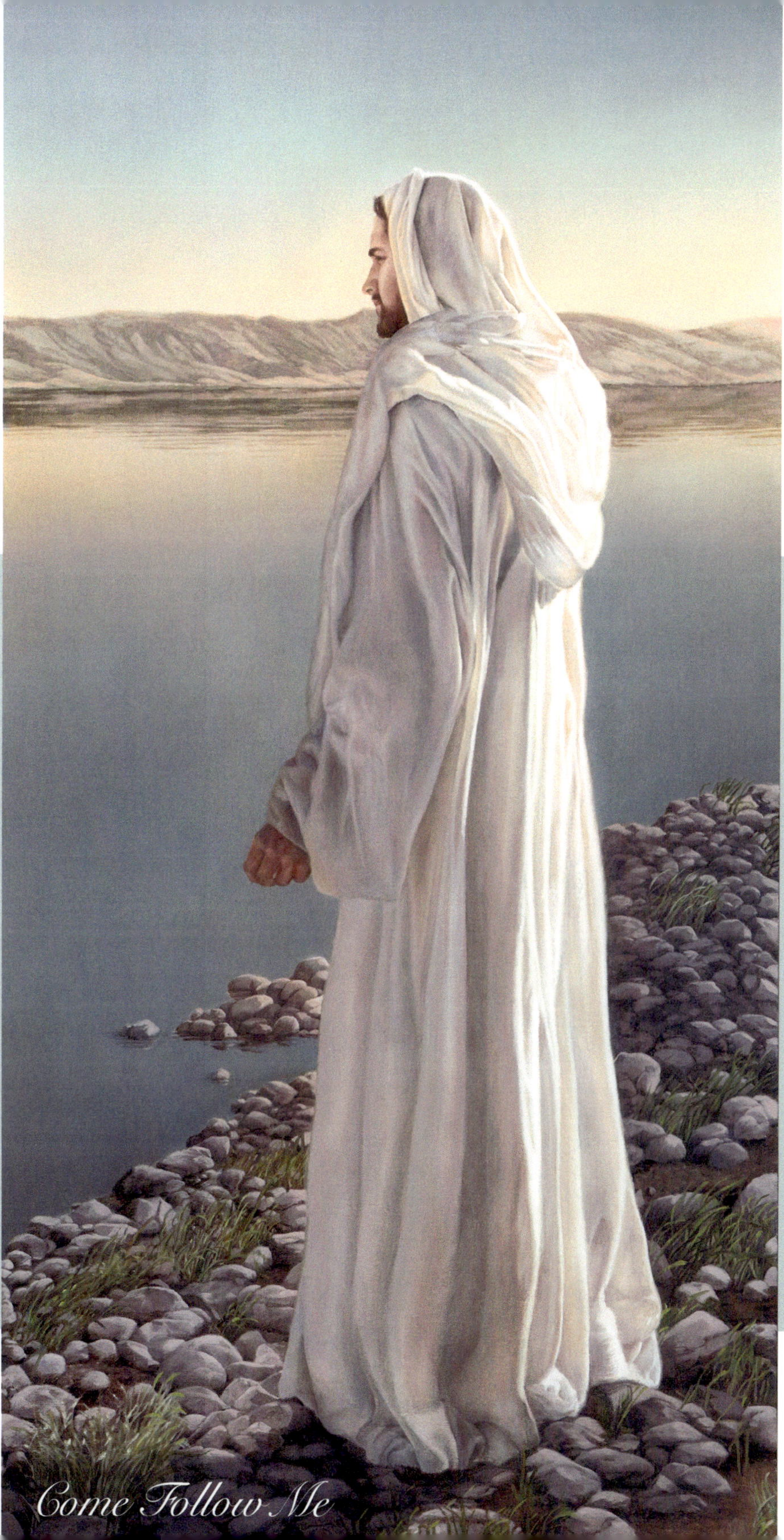
Come Follow Me

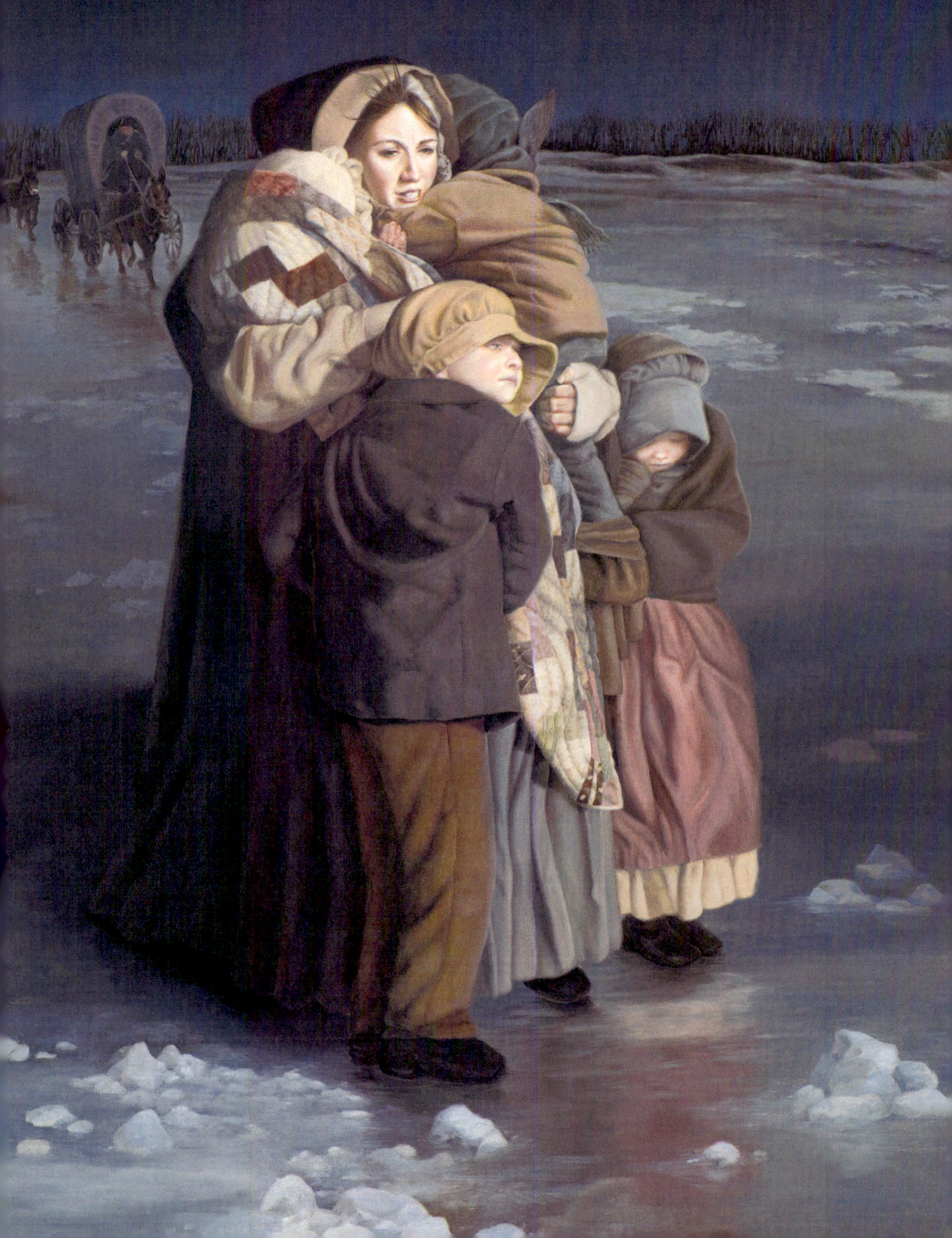

Emma on the Ice

The Saints had fled to Far West hoping for a rest from their enemies, but the growing mob violence resulted in the imprisonment of Joseph Smith at Liberty Jail and the slaughter at Haun's Mill. Driven from their homes in the dead of winter, the Saints began the long journey to Nauvoo.

Emma was among the Saints forced to cross the frozen Mississippi River. Can you imagine the faith it must have taken to step on that ice carrying an eight-month-old baby and two-year-old son, while the others clung to her skirts? During those dark days, Joseph wrote, "O God, where art thou? And where is the pavilion that covereth thy hiding place?" (D&C 121:1).

I thought of the pain and sorrow both Joseph and Emma were laboring under at that moment and realized that for Joseph and Emma, though separated by distance, they were truly of one heart.

At those times when I feel alone and forgotten I look at this painting and remember that nothing in mortality can place us beyond the reach of divinity.

Driving through a parking lot, I saw a boy and his father coming out of a store. The boy was imagining himself as a mighty hero, but he looked at his father with more admiration than any hero is likely to receive. Right then, I knew I had to paint "Even Superman Needs a Dad."

This father took an interest in everything his son had to say. Every moment seemed magical. While this little boy looked a bit out of place dressed in a Superman cape and red cowboy boots, his father could not have looked prouder. Who was the real Hero? Who was more in awe of whom?

When I look around at the thousands of Supermen who play alone each day, it breaks my heart. Looking at these two, I remember a wonderful father who took the time to be there for me, who taught me by example what a father should be.

I enjoy watching someone look at the painting for the first time. Their gradual smile tells me they understand the feeling that brought about this painting. For a brief moment, they forget there are bills to pay and work to do. They forget their worries and remember for a moment that life is wonderful. That is the joy in painting.

Even Superman Needs a Dad

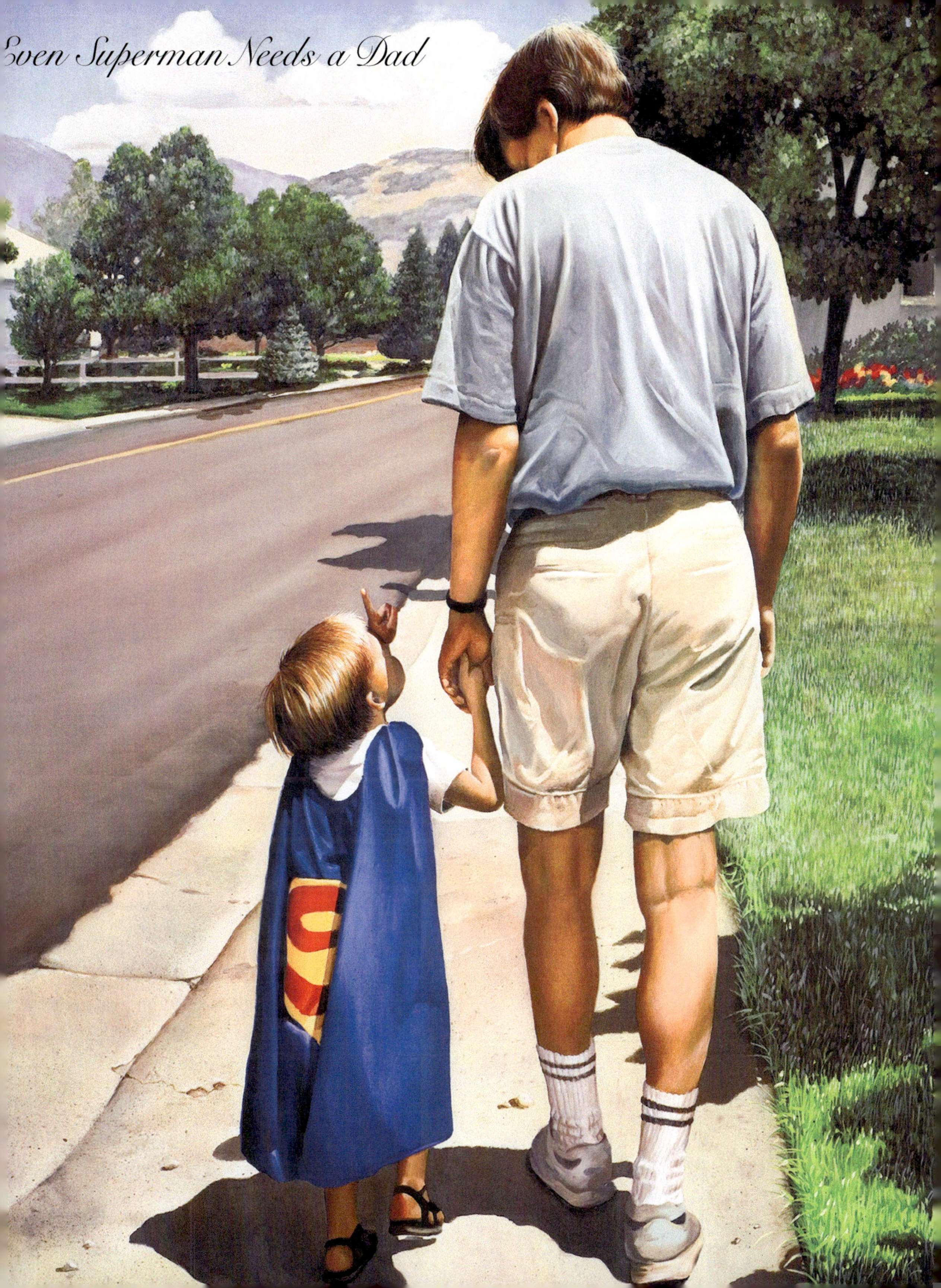

In each of our lives we are faced with confusion. Decisions can be difficult when the answers are unclear. At fourteen years old, Joseph Smith was faced with a country torn by religious revivalism. Preachers of all sects clamored for converts in a battle for men's very souls. Joseph recounts the following: "So great were the confusion and strife among the different denominations, that it was impossible for a person young as I was, and so unacquainted with men and things, to come to any certain conclusion who was right and who was wrong" (Joseph Smith—History 1:8).

Joseph continued to search for answers to his confusion. One evening, Joseph was reading the family Bible in the book of James, first chapter and fifth verse: "If any of you lack wisdom, let him ask of God, that giveth to all men liberally, and upbraideth not; and it shall be given him." Joseph arrived at the conclusion that he must either remain in darkness or ask God which of all the churches was God's church.

His humble prayer was answered on a beautiful morning, early in the spring of 1820. God the Father and His Son Jesus Christ appeared to the young boy Joseph Smith in a quiet grove of trees. This began the Restoration of the Lord's kingdom upon the earth. God had spoken to men again, and the silence of the heavens was shattered.

This event confirms the reality of the Savior of the world, Jesus Christ, for Joseph saw Him standing on the right hand of God. This remarkable vision provides the answer for the honest in heart who seek to know God's truth.

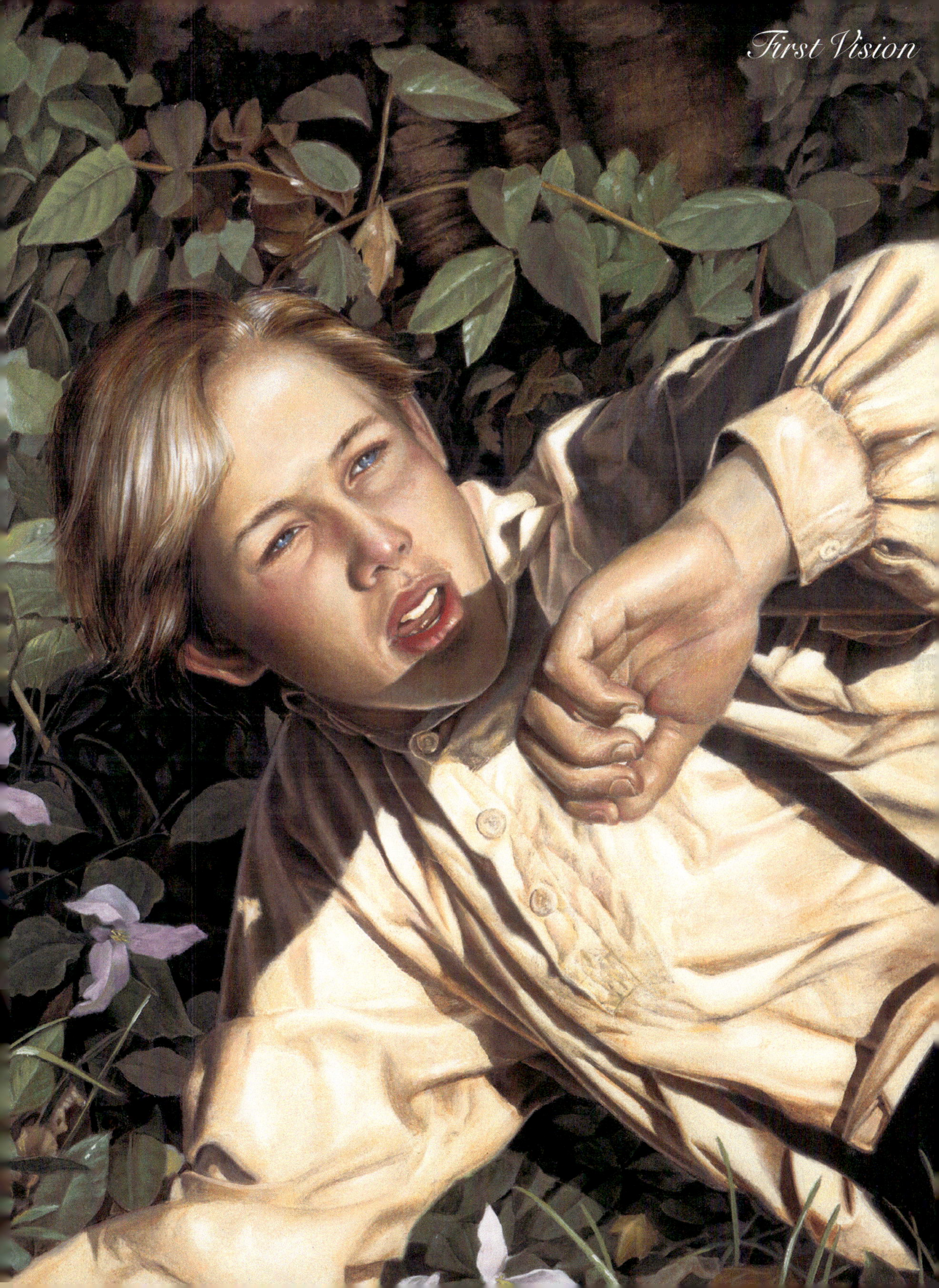

First Vision

One of the first children I met in Zambia was a little boy named Kennedy. At three years old, Kennedy had lost both of his parents to AIDS and was found living alone with his six-year-old brother and ten-year-old sister. When I thought of those three children struggling to survive and the millions of others across Africa in similar circumstances, I felt an overwhelming hopelessness and said to myself, "No amount of money can fix this."

I was curious to see how Kennedy and the others would react to Phillip, the man playing Christ. We decided to drop Phillip off several hundred yards from the "farm" and then drive in and set up our cameras. We told the children we had a wonderful surprise for them. When Phillip came into view, the children instinctively ran to him and threw their arms around him. Everyone except Kennedy.

When Phillip saw this little boy standing apart from the others, he walked over and knelt down. As he opened his arms, this little soul ran to him and he threw his arms around Phillip's neck. He began speaking as fast as he could. Phillip looked for help to understand. One of the others translated:

"My mom and dad died. They are in heaven. Have you seen them? Are they okay?"

At that moment I knew it wasn't hopeless. I realized that the Savior could fix not only the problems of Africa, but of the whole world . . . and we can be His hands to do it. For the first time in my life, I felt what Isaiah meant when he said, "He will swallow up death in victory; and the Lord God will wipe away tears from off all faces" (Isaiah 25:8). To Kennedy and all who struggle to understand *why*, I promise that God has not forgotten you; that the time is coming when He will come in power and glory and when He will keep his promise and wipe away all of our tears.

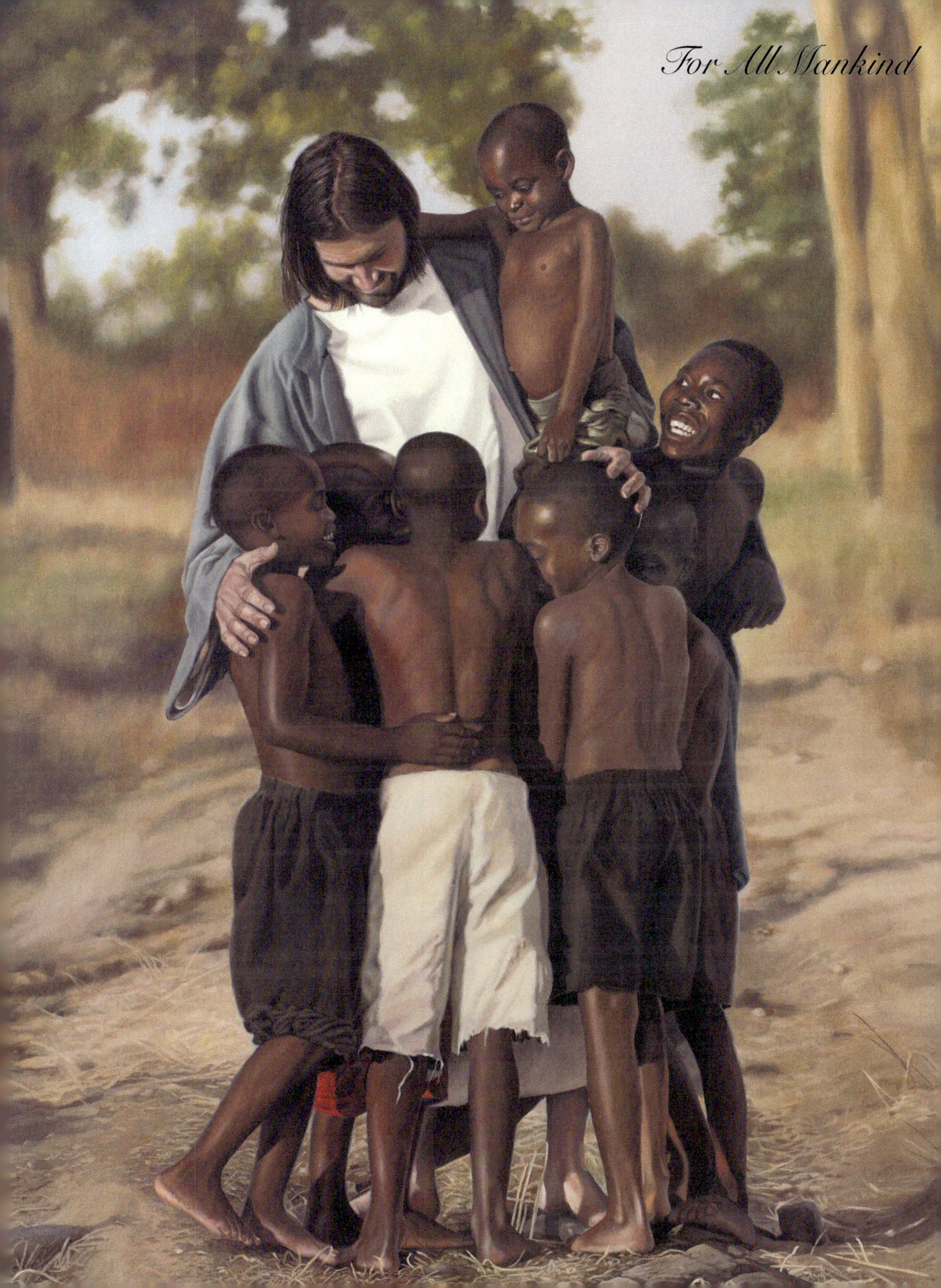

For All Mankind

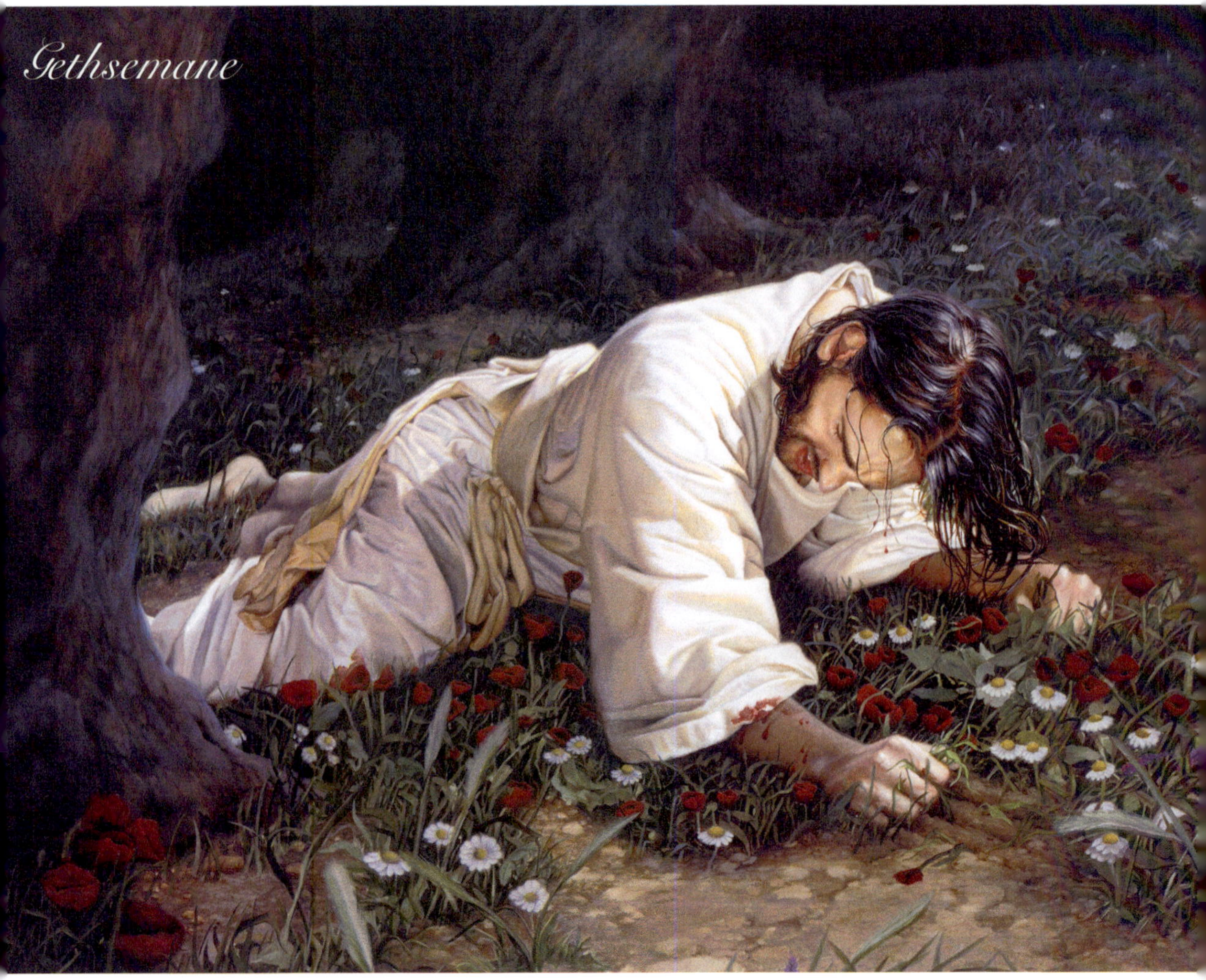
Gethsemane

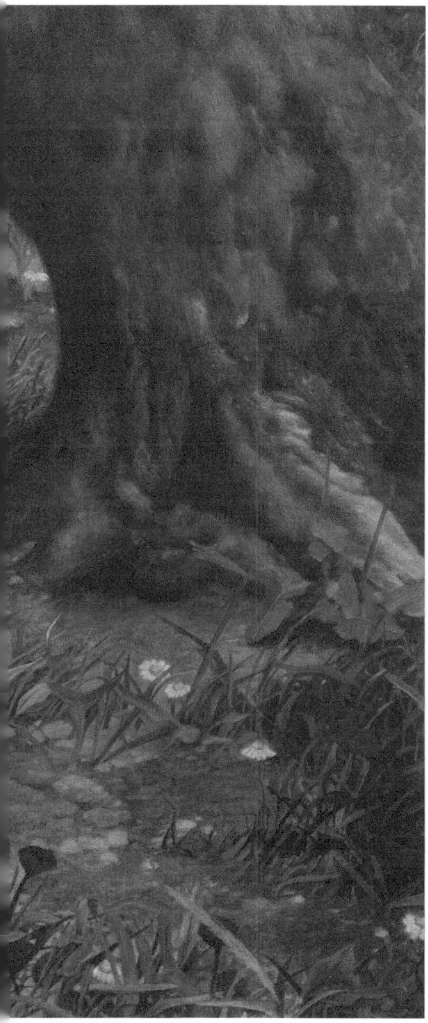

When I started this painting, I believed that Gethsemane was about the suffering of Christ—about the agony so intense that He trembled because of pain and bled from every pore. By the time I finished, I saw that the miracle of Gethsemane went beyond the suffering; the miracle was the love that brought Him there.

"For God so loved the world, that he gave his only begotten Son, that whosoever believeth in him should not perish, but have everlasting life. For God sent not his Son into the world to condemn the world; but that the world through him might be saved" (John 3:16–17).

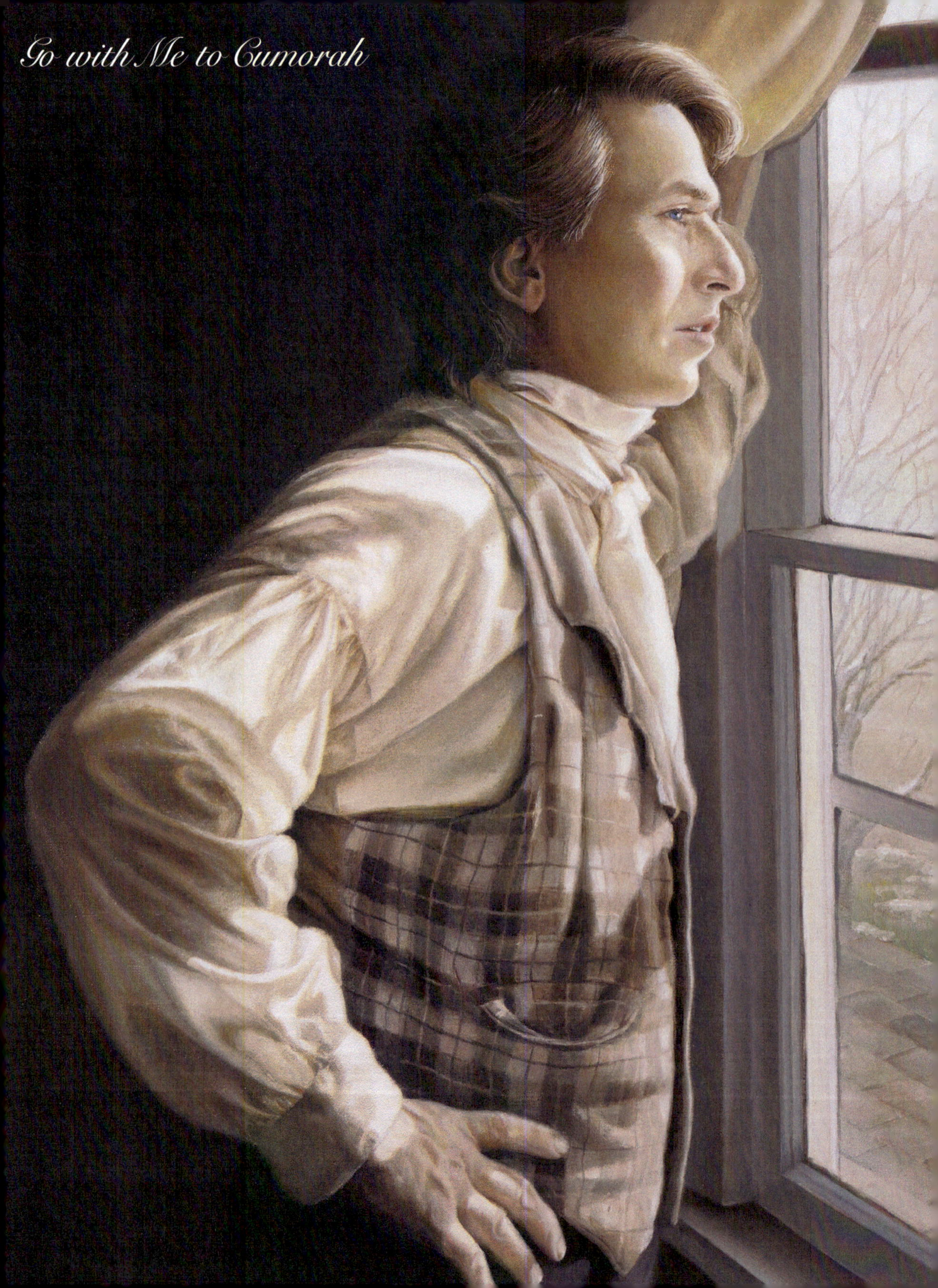

Go with Me to Cumorah

In the spring of 1820, Joseph walked from his parent's home to a grove of trees to pray. His humble prayer brought an appearance of the Father and the Son and started a new dispensation of truth.

In 1831, the persecutions of the Saints in Palmyra had just begun. Joseph knew the persecution would only increase; so with sadness in his heart the they prepared to leave for Kirtland, Ohio.

I thought about the times I have moved; the quiet moments when you pause to remember as you pack something; the last look back as you pull away.

I could see Joseph pausing to look at the grove one last time—remembering the moment when it all began.

This project required photographing many situations with Joseph and children. Several accounts in early Church history demonstrate that Joseph loved children and took many opportunities to foster his relationship with them. He was known to have wrestled, participated in snowball fights, pulled sticks, played ball, and fished with the youth. Many children, and especially the LDS boys, recorded looking to Joseph as a hero and a role model. I cannot imagine a better role model for children than the Prophet Joseph Smith.

It strikes me that you cannot truly follow someone you do not know. When I think of my own relationship with my Savior, it becomes clear to me that when He said "Come follow me," He was inviting me to know Him. I am convinced that He loves each of us in such a personal way that He is overjoyed when we come to know Him and sorrows when we make Him a stranger. Joseph is an example of someone who knew the Savior and followed Him.

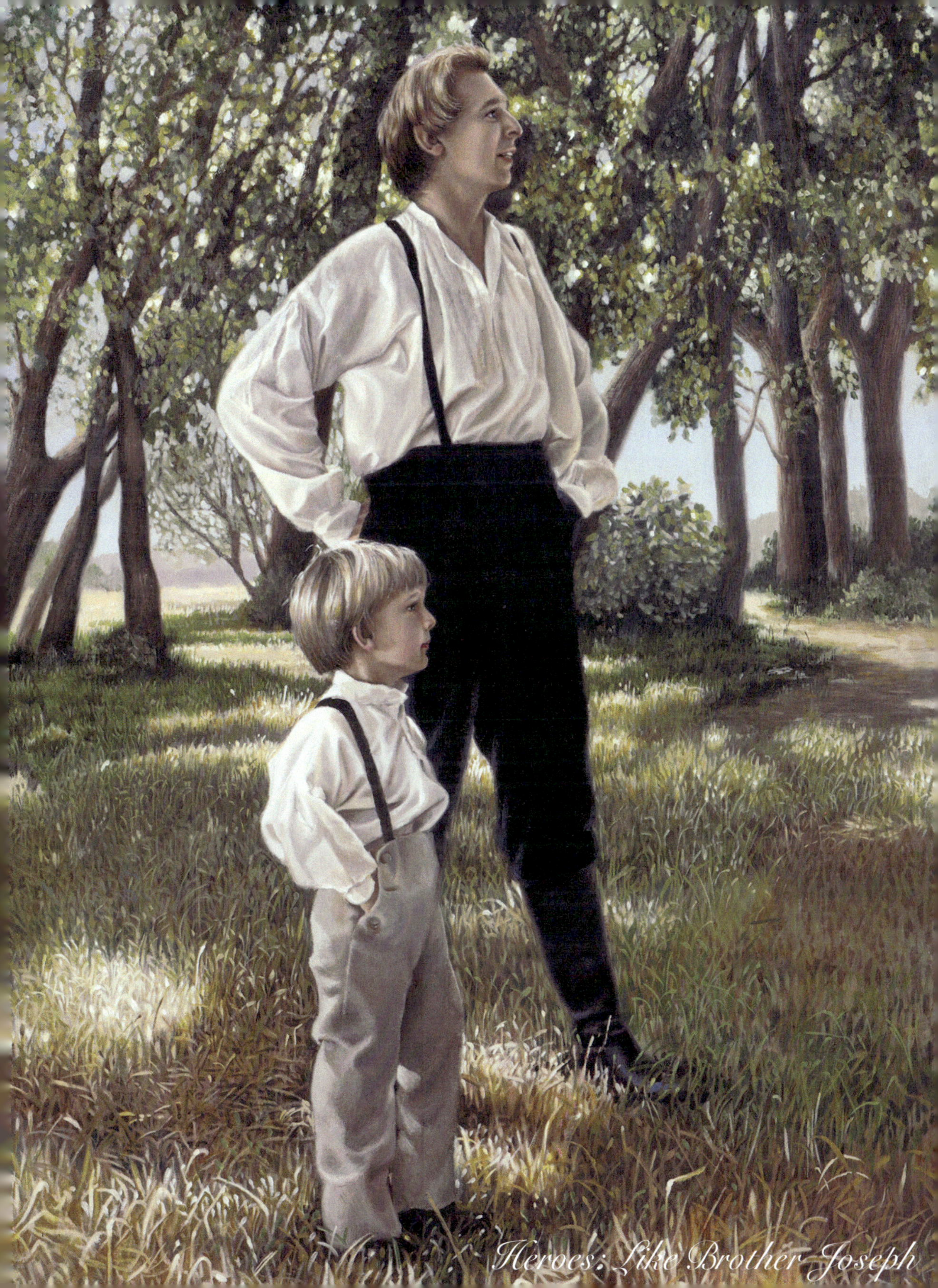
Heroes: Like Brother Joseph

Heroes: Like Nephi of Old

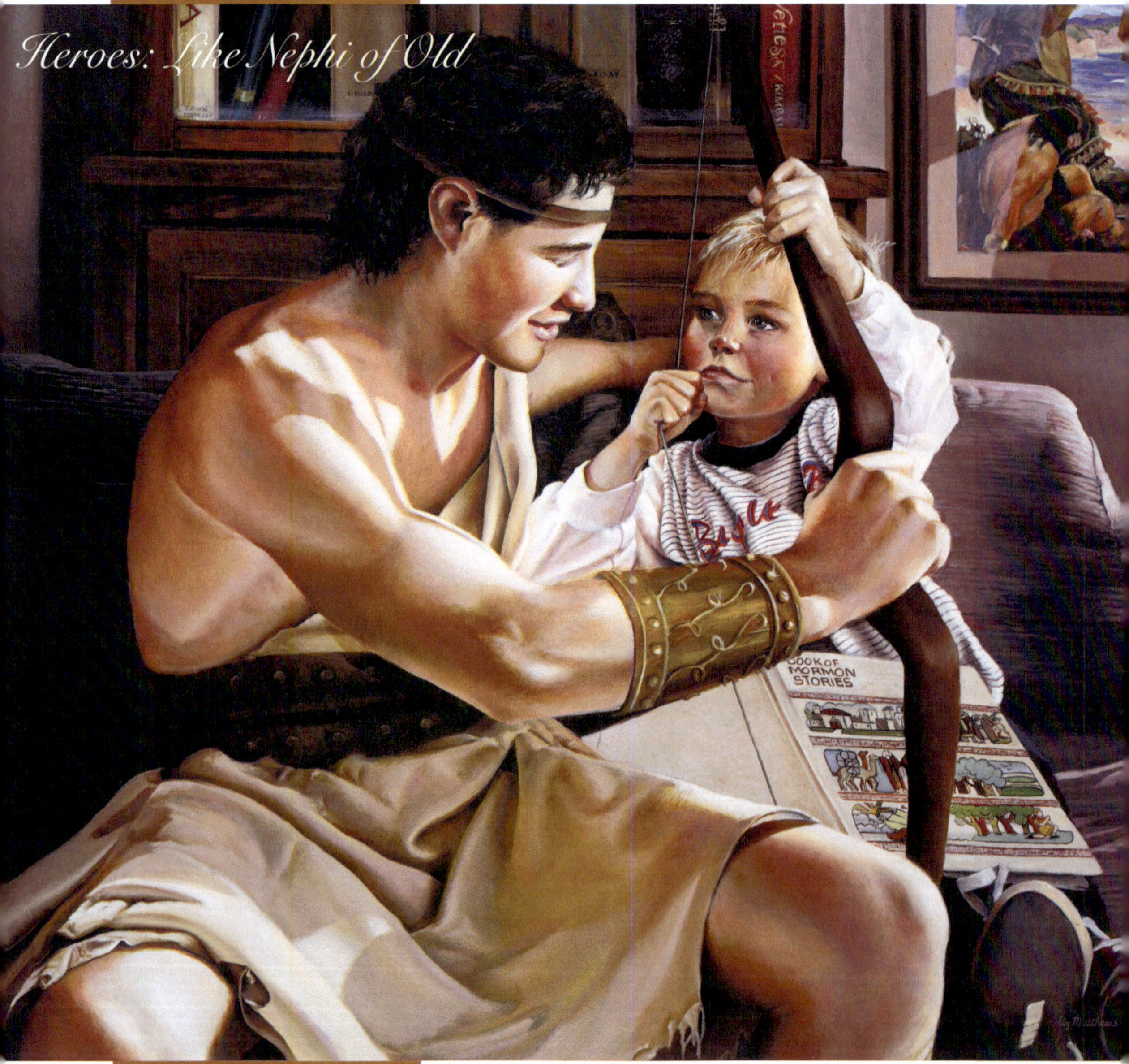

The painting "Heroes: Like Nephi of Old" began in the summer of 1991. My original idea was a picture of a father and his young son reading the Book of Mormon. I asked a young boy, Nathan, to model for the painting.

Before we started, we talked about his favorite Book of Mormon characters and Nathan told me about Nephi. When Nathan spoke of him, he talked as if Nephi lived next door. The longer I listened, the more I came to understand that Nathan truly knew Nephi. "Heroes: Like Nephi of Old" emerged from this experience.

Listening to Nathan started me thinking about how close the heroes of the past are to those who listen. As I look around, I am reminded that we clearly live in a world where righteousness is seldom the standard by which heroes are measured.

Nathan reminded me that heroes are only heroes if they give more than they take, lift more than they hinder, and love more than they hurt. Nathan taught me that our greatest heroes never emerge from the pages of a comic book, but are found in our past.

Saying "Hold on tight!" is what anyone might say when carrying a child piggyback. Jesus loved and enjoyed children, and probably played with them from time to time. It is not hard to imagine a group of children trying to get His attention and one feeling very special riding high on His back.

The direction to "hold on tight" may also be taken metaphorically—do we follow His teachings with all of our might? His teachings and commandments were given to help us avoid problems and ultimately be happy. The message is as simple as the painting; Christ wants us to be happy simply because He loves us.

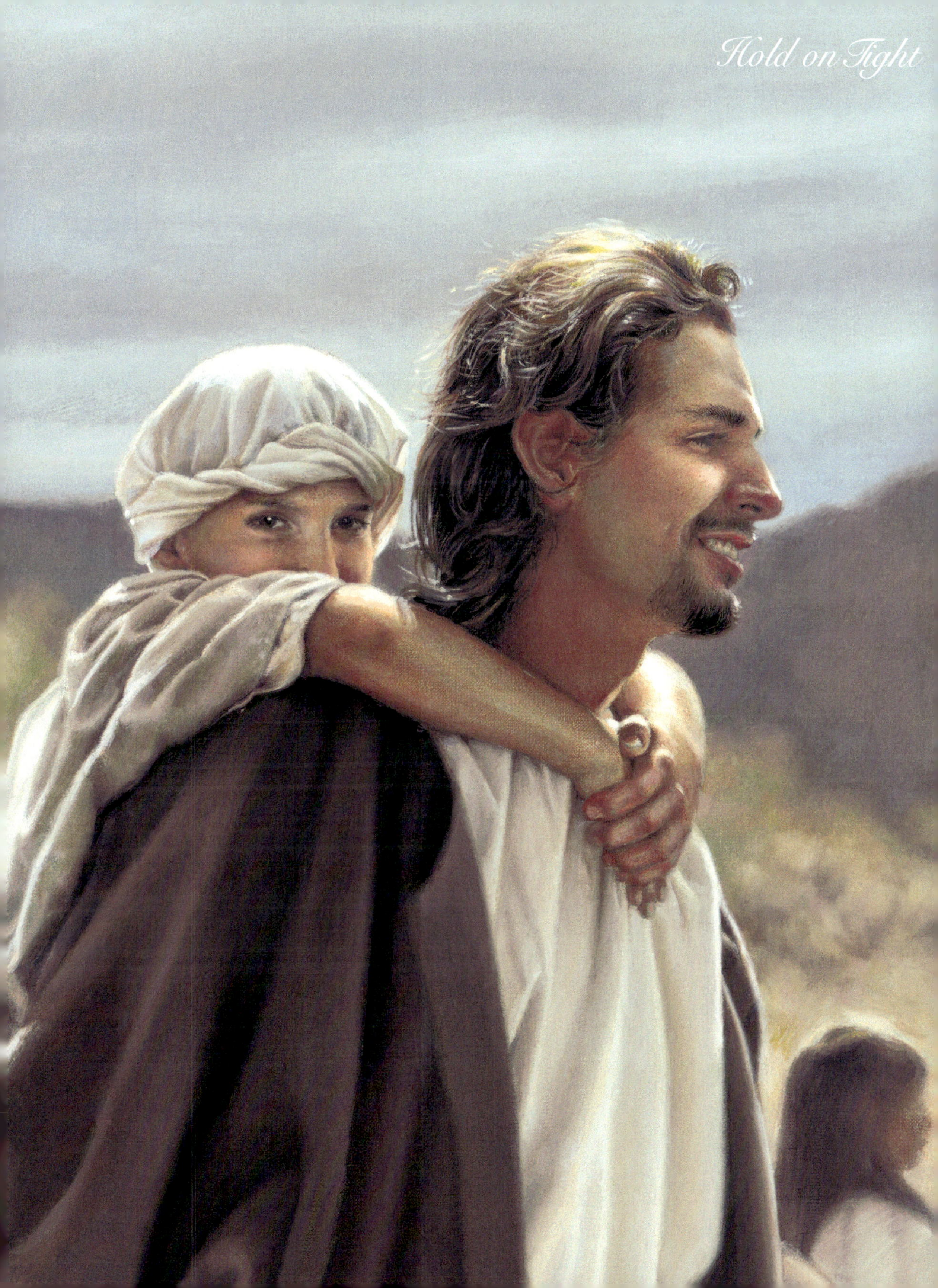
Hold on Tight

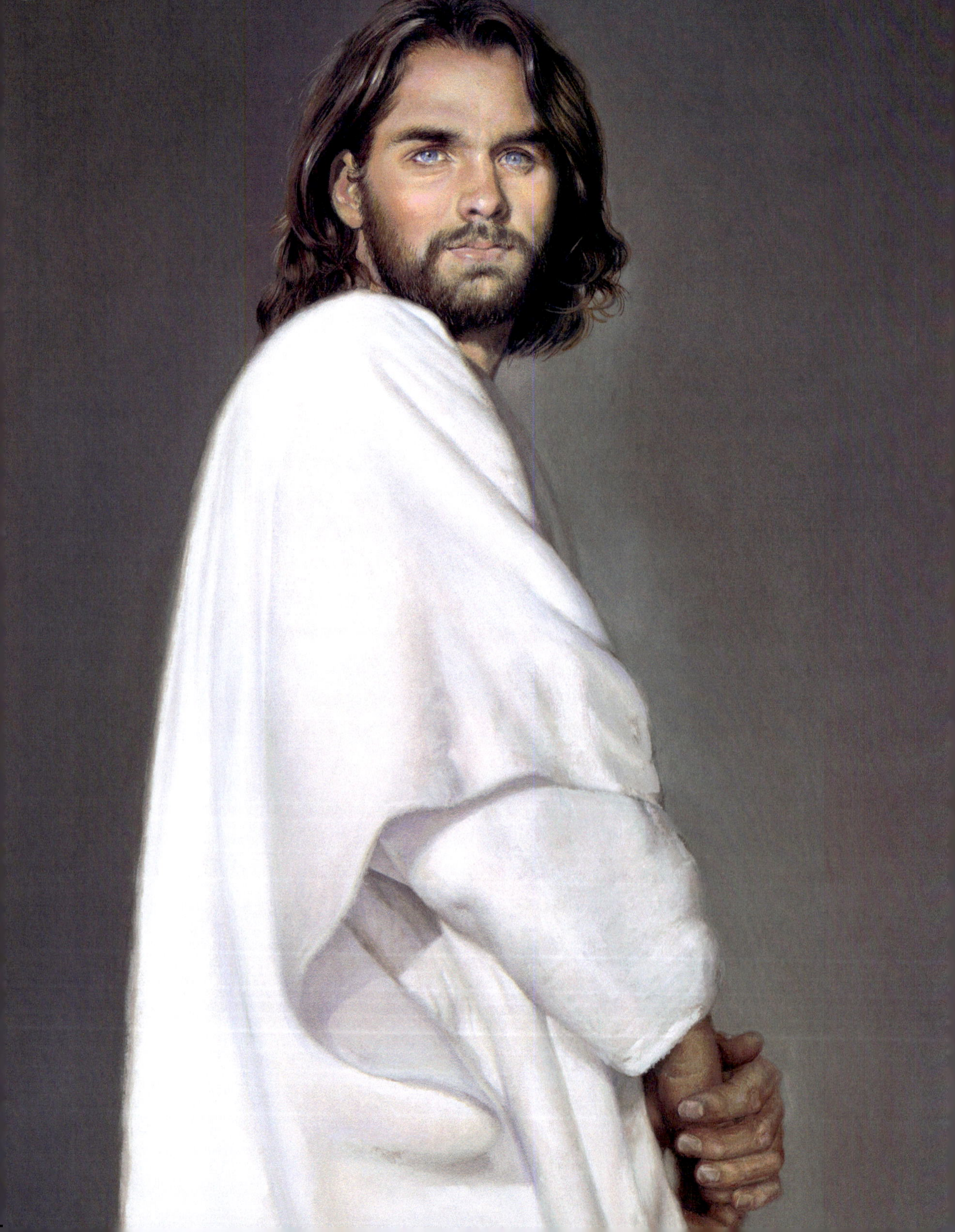

Jesus

When I began painting the life of Christ, I promised myself that I would paint a portrait of the Savior each year. I wanted to see how my view of the Savior would change as I came to know Him better.

This was the first portrait. It gets its name from my two-year-old granddaughter. I came into my studio one morning to find her standing in front of the painting. She was carrying on a conversation and as I listened I could make out the word "Jesus."

The Bible contains a single verse describing the Savior's childhood: "And the child grew, and waxed strong in spirit, filled with wisdom: and the grace of God was upon him" (Luke 2:40).

I could imagine Mary looking on while her Son played with His brothers and sisters (see Matthew 13:55–56). I could see Joseph smiling while Jesus laughed and played with friends and family. I wanted to capture that magical innocence of childhood, which blesses our lives for such a short moment and then leaves us longing for the sound of little feet and the laughter of little children.

I am reminded of a song I learned as little girl:

Jesus once was a little child,
A little child like me;
And he was pure and meek and mild,
As a little child should be.

So, little children,
Let's you and I
Try to be like him,
Try, try, try.

("Jesus Once Was a Little Child," *Children's Songbook*, 55.)

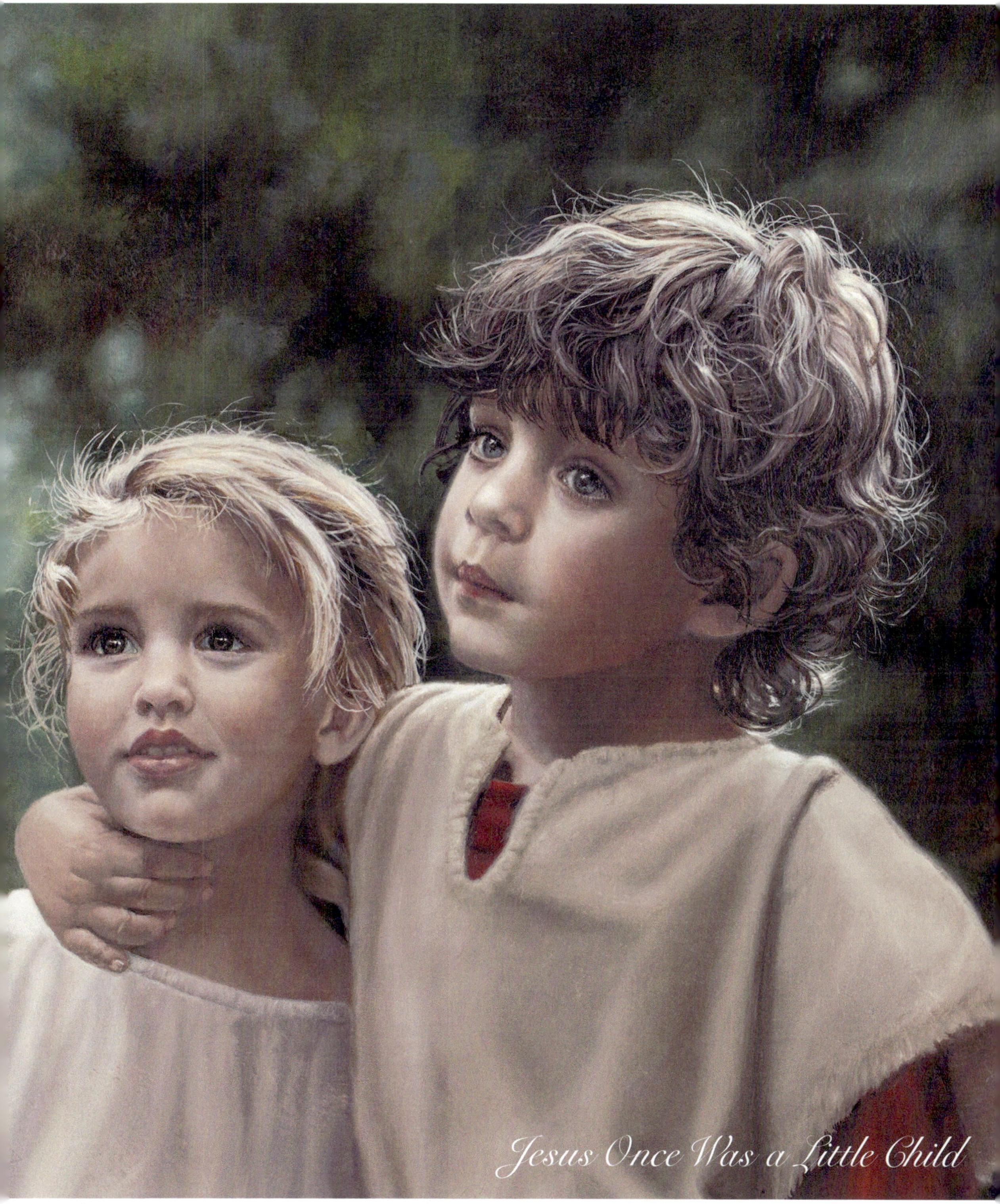
Jesus Once Was a Little Child

Too often we look on the Savior as distant and removed from us. We remember Him as the God of the Universe possessing all power and might, yet forget that He is our personal Savior.

I painted this piece because I wanted to try and change the way my children and grandchildren thought of Jesus Christ. I wanted them to think of Him as a friend and the first One they turn to for peace and comfort. I wanted Him to be for them a light shining in the darkness.

In trying to change my children's perception, I changed my own. Each time I look at this painting I find myself smiling. I think He would like that.

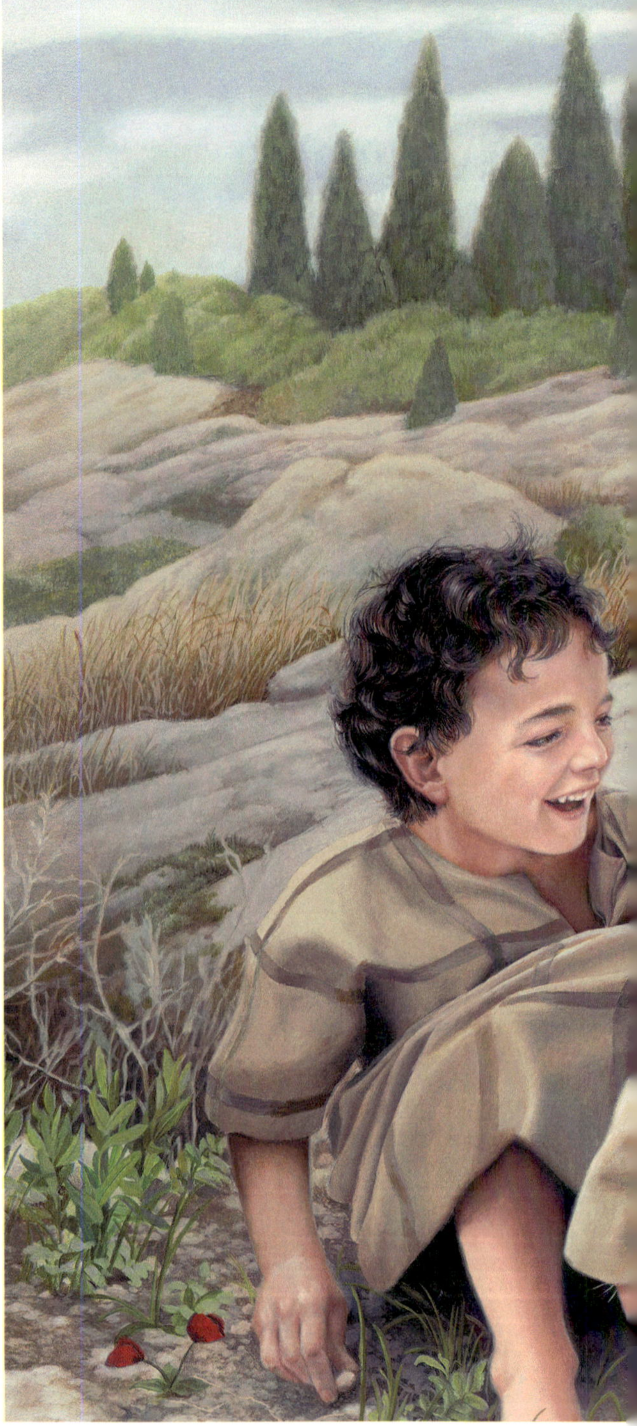

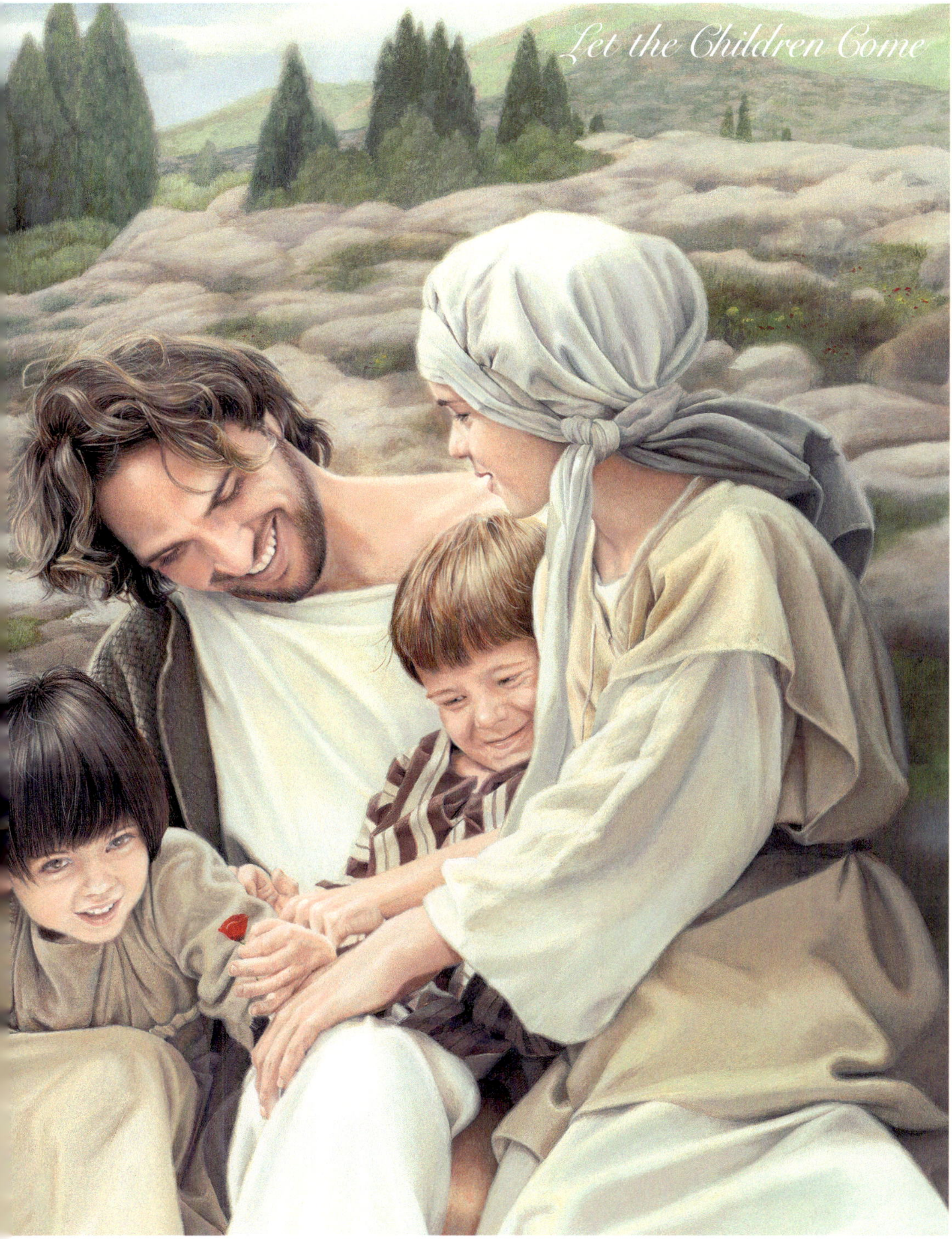
Let the Children Come

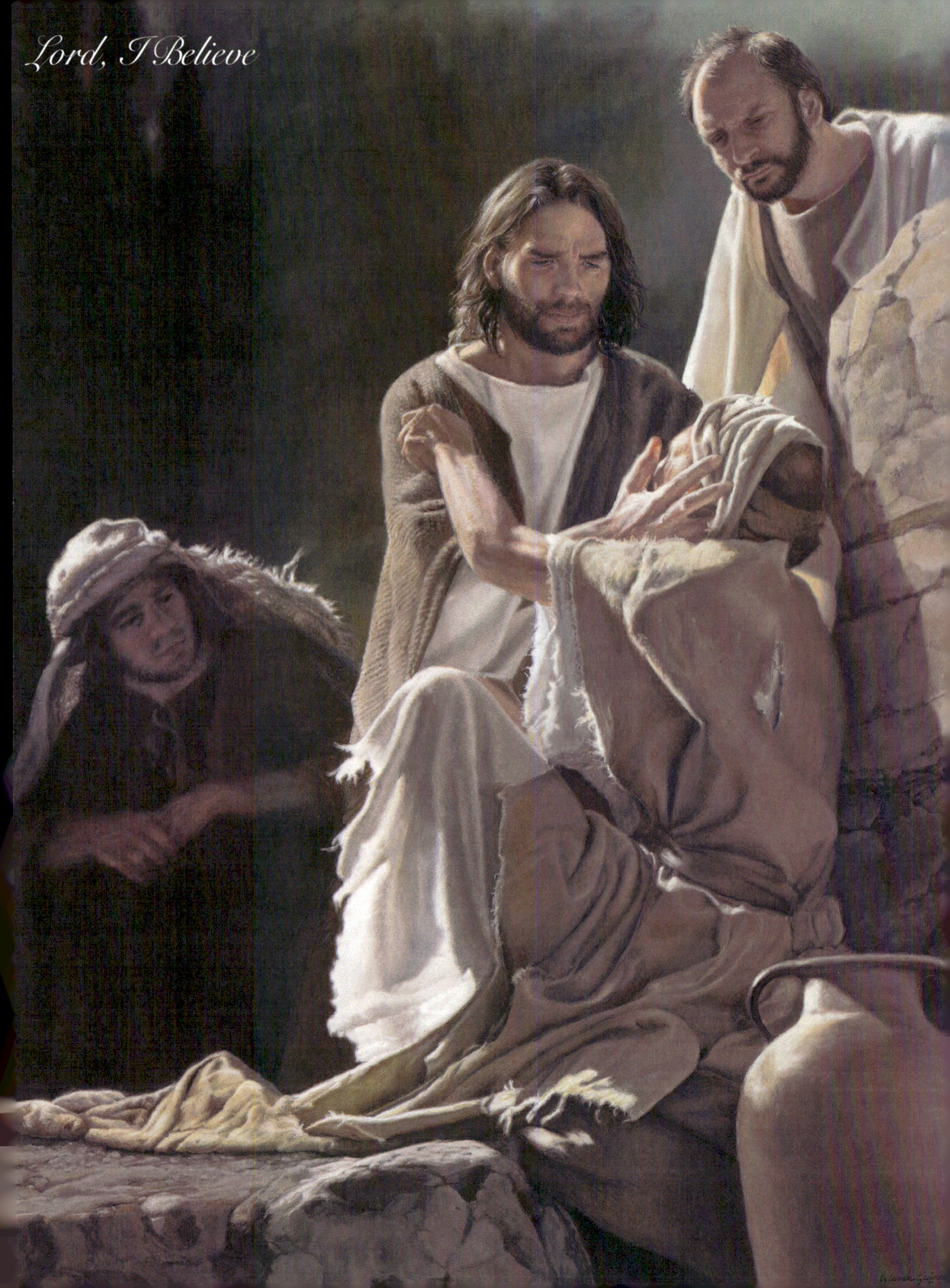
Lord, I Believe

This painting has special meaning to me. My son was diagnosed with diabetes when he was seven years old. I have watched the disease ravage his body always knowing in the back of my mind that one day it would overtake him. I just didn't know it would be so soon. When I heard that his eyesight was failing, my heart sank. I pleaded with the Lord asking for more time. I wanted desperately for him to see his children grow up.

As I painted this piece, I was reminded that although the Lord does not always give us the answers we beg for, He does give us the eyes to see. There are times it feels like He leaves us reaching in the darkness, not sure of the ending. Yet even in our spiritual blindness we feel His hands, holding on to us, healing us. And with new eyes we see Him more clearly and know that even though the miracles may not come as we expect, they will come.

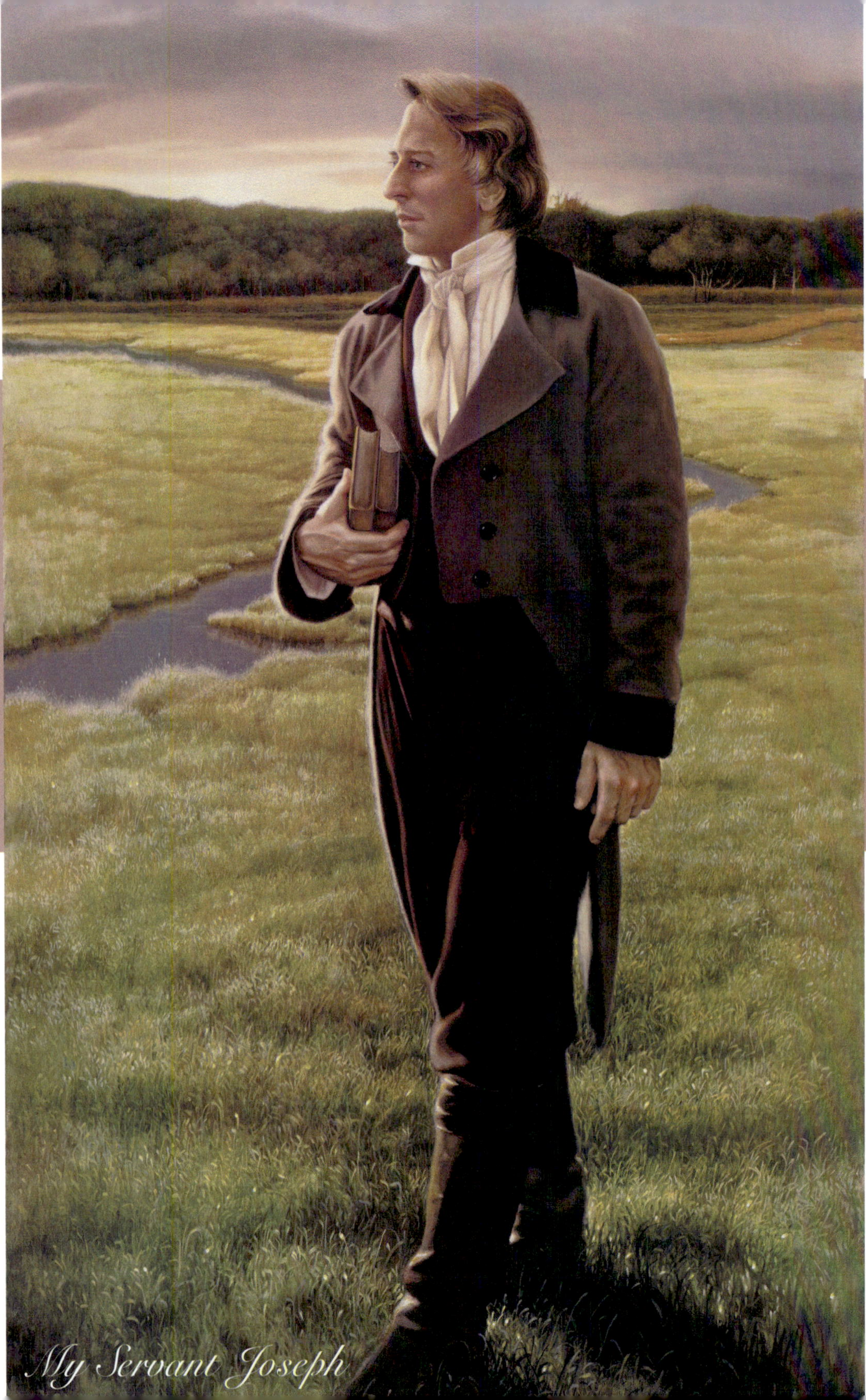
My Servant Joseph

I am continually amazed at how willingly we pass by life's rare moments of inspiration. Unknowingly we turn away from the quiet glimpses of eternity on our way to somewhere else.

It was on my way to somewhere else in my career when I became moved to paint the life of Joseph Smith. Looking back, that one decision has had a more profound impact on my life than almost any other.

I, along with millions of others, believe the words of the Lord, "Wherefore, I the Lord, knowing the calamity which should come upon the inhabitants of the earth, called upon my servant Joseph Smith, Jun., and spake unto him from heaven" (D&C 1:17).

This is the second painting I did of the Prophet Joseph Smith. When I started this painting I thought I knew who Joseph Smith was. Looking back, I realize I knew things about him, but I did not know him.

I started seeing the human side of Joseph when I understood he cared more for his brother's life than his own. When Joseph decided to return to Carthage and stand trial, Hyrum insisted on coming with him. Joseph must have known he was going to die; I am sure he wanted to protect Hyrum. But Hyrum followed Joseph in death just as he had followed him in life.

Of this moment, John Taylor said:

"Immediately, when the ball struck him, [Hyrum] fell flat on his back, crying as he fell, 'I am a dead man!' He never moved afterwards. I shall never forget the deep feeling of sympathy and regard manifested in the countenance of Brother Joseph as he drew nigh to Hyrum and leaning over him exclaimed, "Oh! My poor, dear brother Hyrum!"

What a price was paid for the gospel. May we never forget.

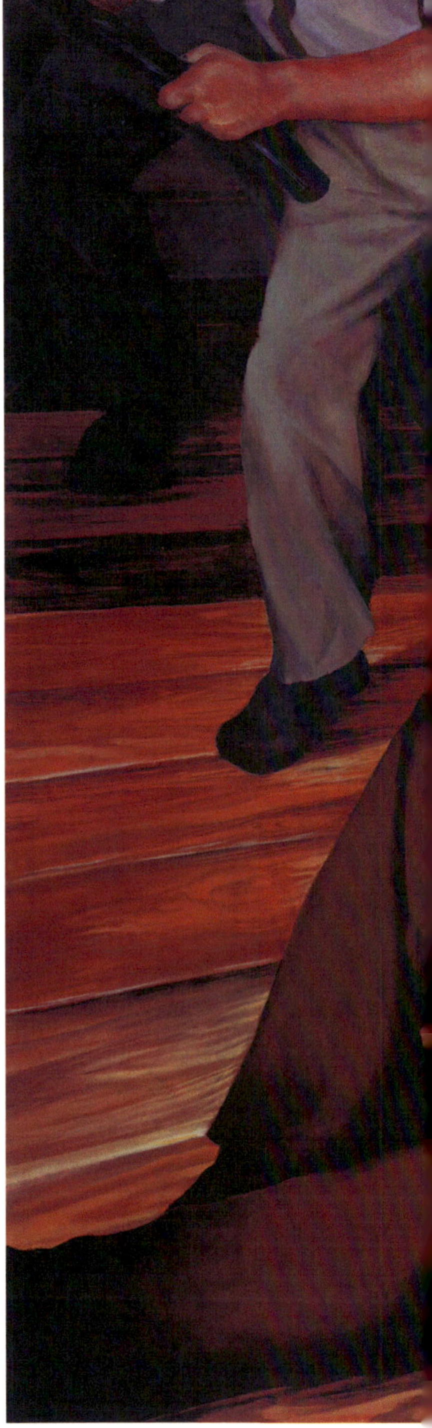

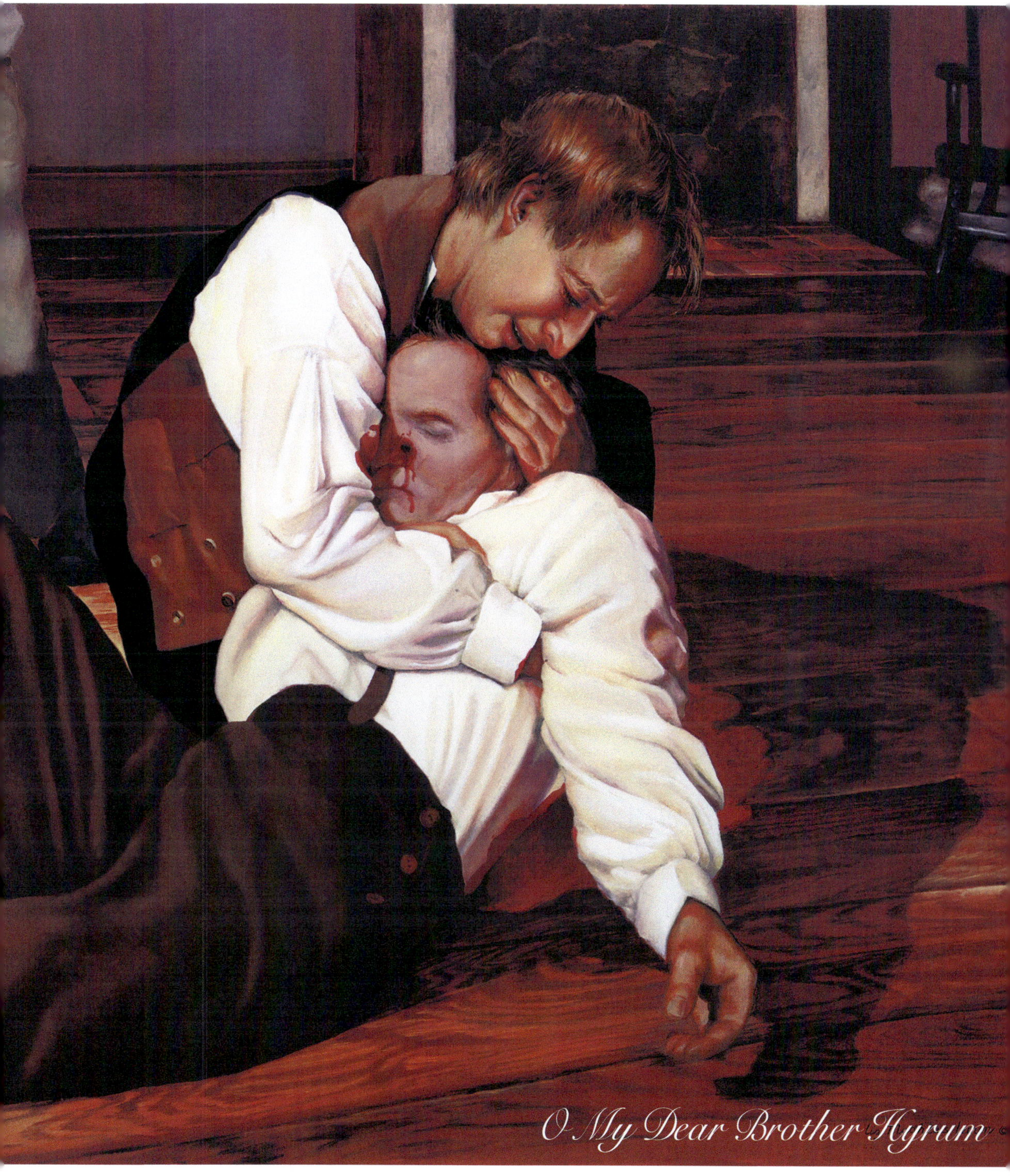
O My Dear Brother Hyrum

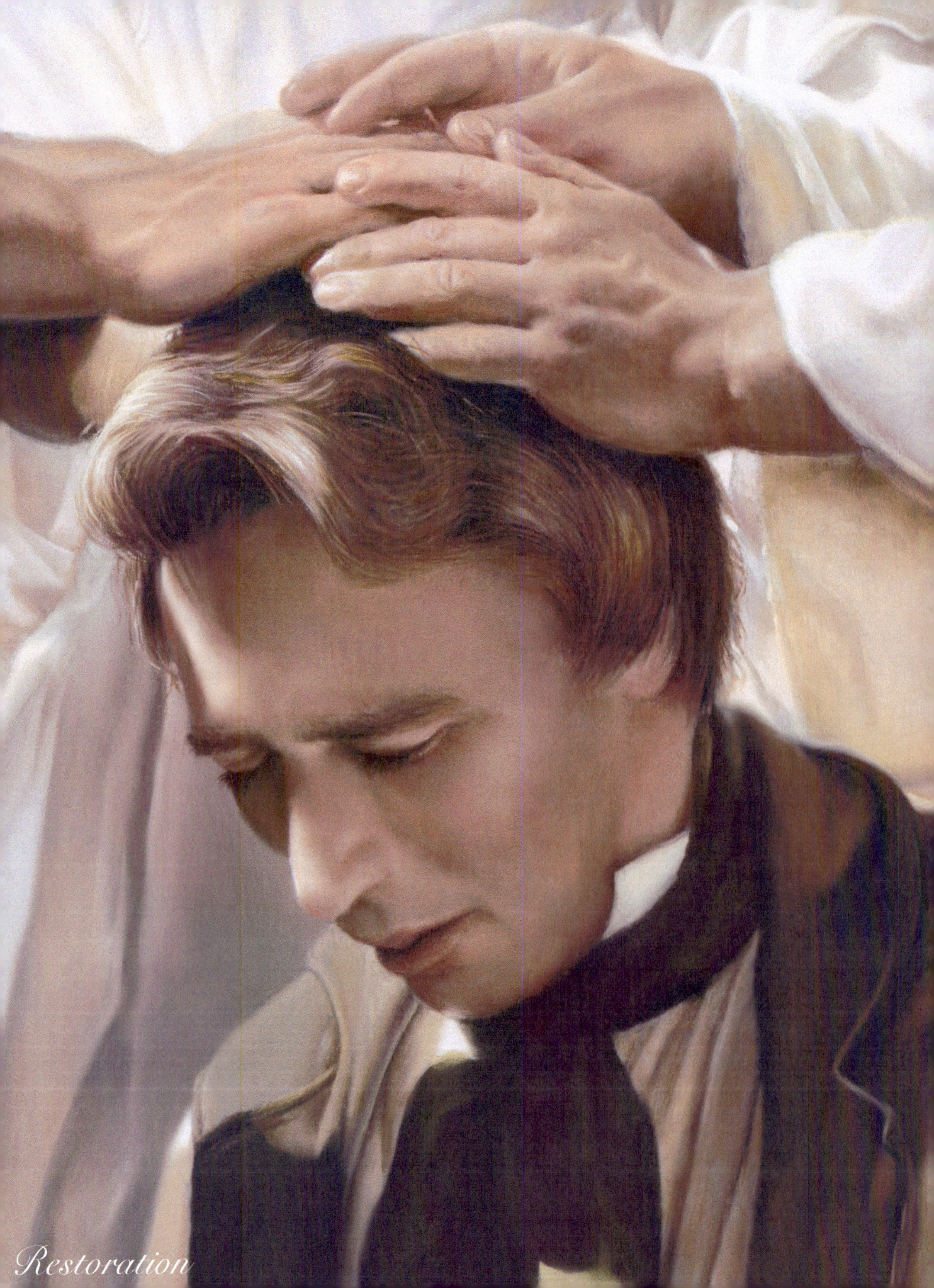

Restoration

Shortly after receiving the Aaronic Priesthood, Joseph and Oliver were returning home to Harmony when the Lord's chief Apostles, Peter, James, and John, appeared to them on the banks of the Susquehanna River. They conferred upon Joseph and Oliver the holy Melchizedek Priesthood and the keys of apostleship. Joseph and Oliver now had the authority to act as legal agents for the Lord in building the kingdom of God upon the earth.

I am struck by the magnitude of this event; for thousands of years, the world had struggled in darkness. Christ's Church was no longer on the earth; yet righteous men and women around the world struggled to find it. Our Father in Heaven must have wept at the sight of millions of His children searching for truth and knowing that the time was not yet ripe for the Restoration of all things. I think how hard it is for me as a parent to see my children wanting something and knowing that I could not give it. With the hands of Peter, James, and John came hope to a hopeless world.

I thought of how God had answered millions of prayers offered over thousands of years. Our Father in Heaven had again opened the heavens and restored His authority, and with it, His Church. Our Father is indeed merciful to His children.

What we think of as patience may actually be perspective. The ability to see things as they really are gives us the courage to wait upon the Lord even when life takes unexpected turns. The story of the road to Emmaus illustrates this principle beautifully.

Three days after the Savior's death, two of His disciples walked the dusty road from Jerusalem to Emmaus. As they spoke, they were joined by a traveler who asked about their conversation. The disciples replied, "Art thou only a stranger in Jerusalem . . . they have crucified [Jesus]. But we trusted that it had been he which should have redeemed Israel."

Then the stranger said, "Ought not Christ to have suffered these things, and to enter into his glory?" He then opened the scriptures to them, showing how all of the prophets had testified that Christ would be crucified and rise on the third day. As night fell, the disciples asked the traveler to join them for a meal. Sitting together, the stranger "took bread, and blessed it, and brake it, and gave to them. And their eyes were opened, and they knew . . . [it was Jesus]" (Luke 24:17–32).

We are often like the disciples. We let the worries of the day keep us from recognizing that the Savior is walking alongside us. We are quick to treat our trials as curses, instead of trusting that with God's perspective, our "curses" may actually be blessings. May we be more willing to wait upon the Lord, and may we see things as they really are as we walk our own roads to Emmaus.

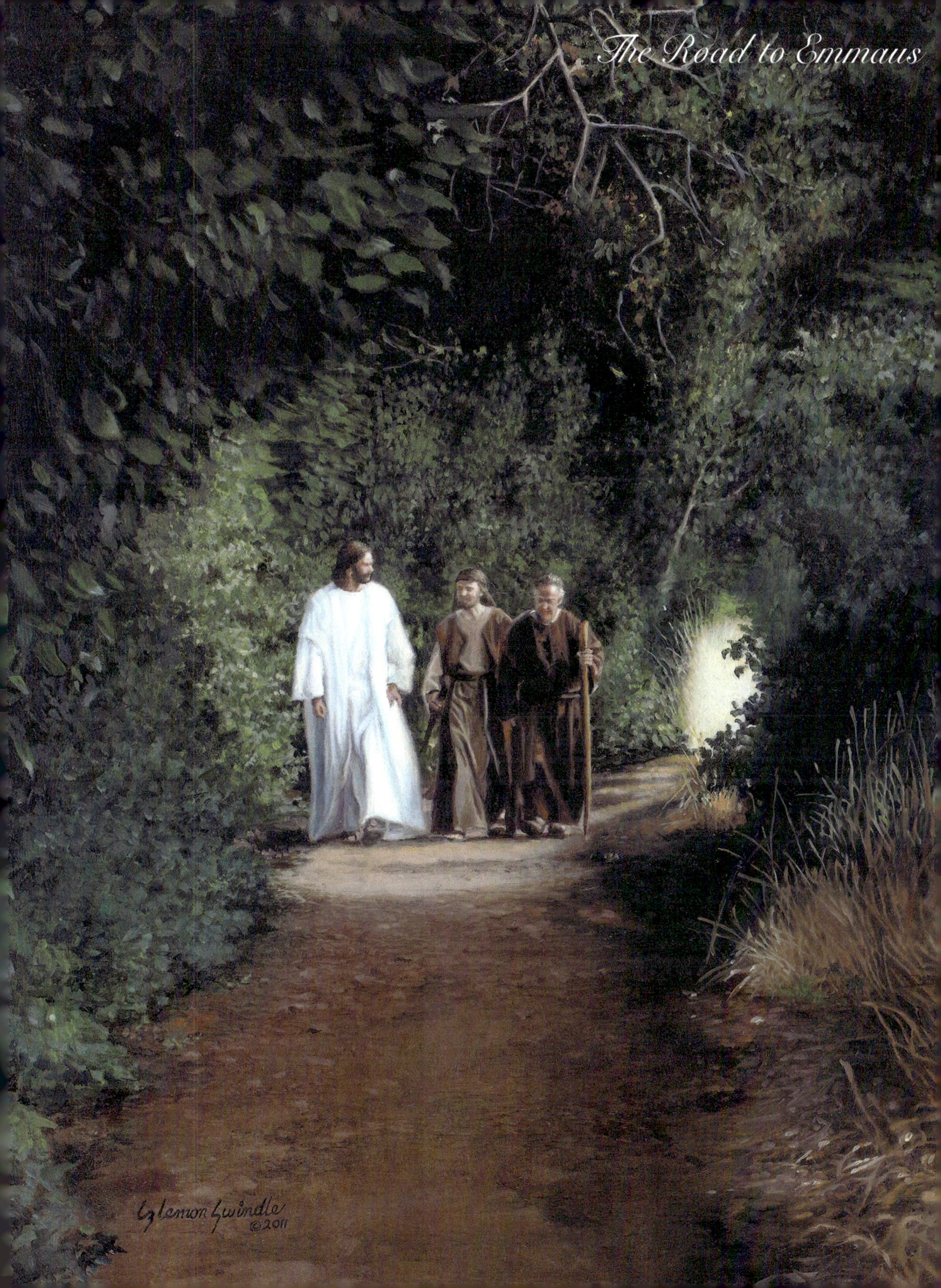
The Road to Emmaus
©2011

In the beginning, my image of Emma was one of sadness. Although my first impression of her is probably accurate to some degree, common sense tells me that not all things are bad all the time. If you live long enough, you come to realize the balance. That holds true for all of us. Nauvoo was the balance. It provided time for the Saints to rest from the past and recharge for the future. Emma had time in Nauvoo to do and be all the things that she had longed for. It was a time to delight in all her roles: Prophet's wife, leader of women, and mother. It was a time of rest and peace and of confidence and laughter.

"To every thing there is a season, and a time to every purpose under the heaven: A time to be born, and a time to die; a time to plant, and a time to pluck up that which is planted; a time to kill, and a time to heal; a time to break down, and a time to build up; a time to weep, and a time to laugh" (Ecclesiastes 3:1–4).

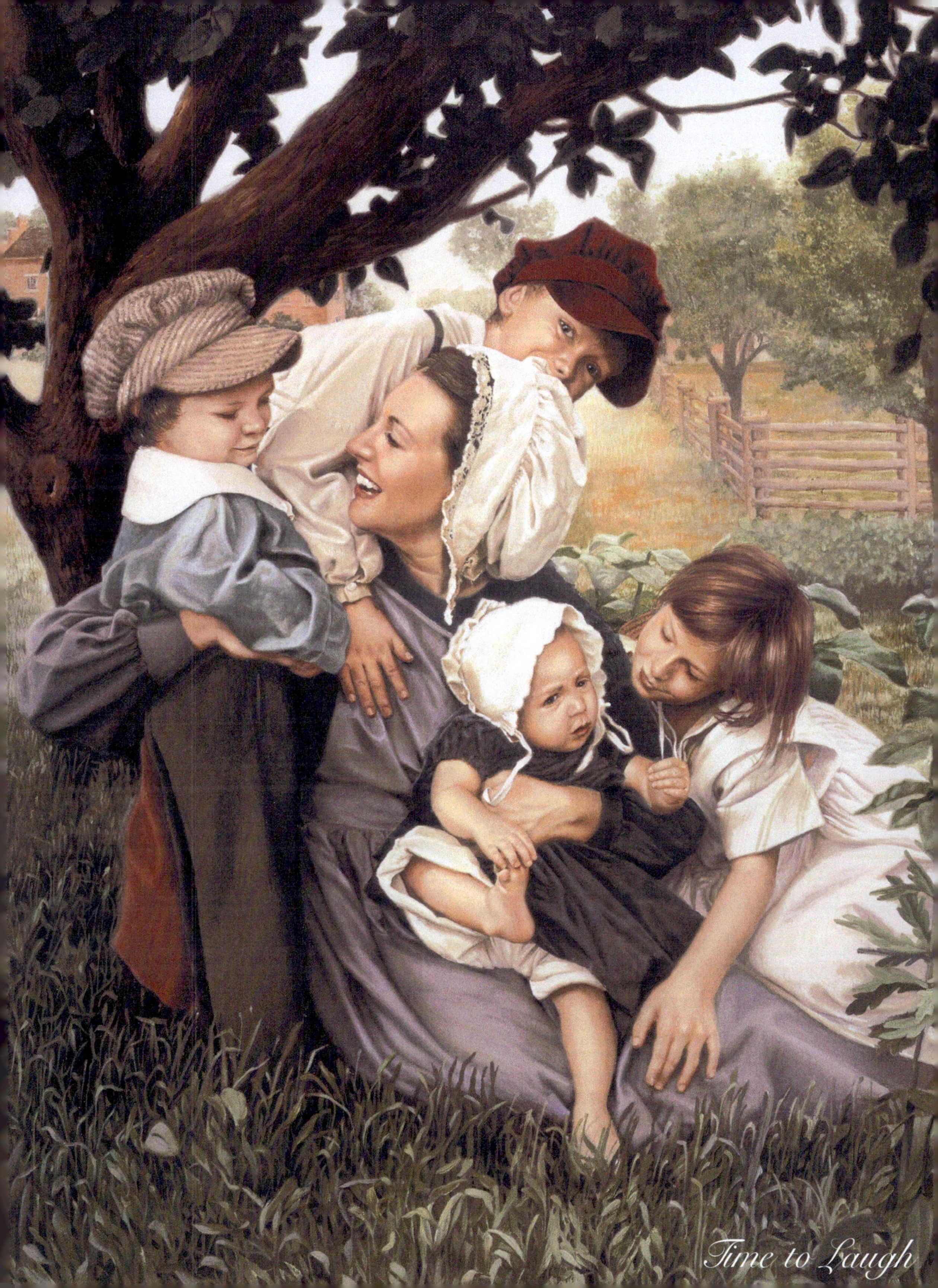
Time to Laugh

Trust in the Lord

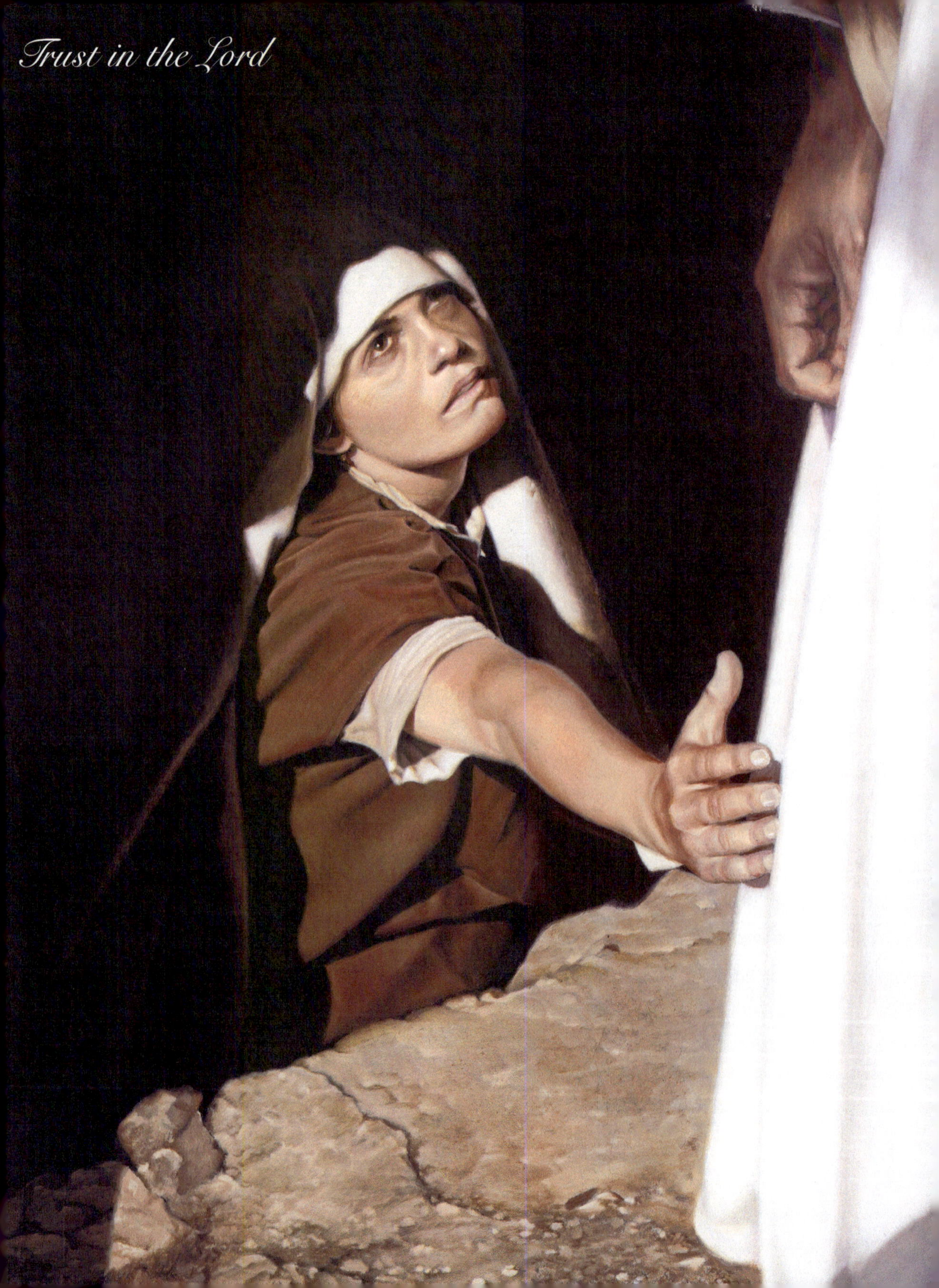

She was considered "unclean" and forced to stay away from others. This means for twelve years she had not had so much as a hug. She knew the risk of going out into public. If discovered, she could have been stoned to death.

Yet her faith led her forward. She had heard of the Savior and the miracles He had already performed. She reached for the Savior with faith that He could heal her, and he did.

This is not so different from each of us. We spend our time on this earth apart from our heavenly home, longing for the company of our Father. We venture into the unknown with little more than hope that the Savior can heal our pains. Like this quiet sister, we reach for Him, and catching hold of Him, we too are healed.

The adopted twins of Joseph and Emma, Joseph and Julia Murdock, were now eleven months old and had been suffering with a difficult case of the measles. Shortly before midnight on March 24, 1832, Joseph sent his exhausted wife to bed with their daughter Julia. Joseph stayed up to care for his infant son, Joseph Murdock, and it wasn't long before they were both asleep.

Suddenly a vicious mob of more than twenty-five men burst through the door, awakening all within and dragging Joseph outside by his hair. Emma ran behind screaming, but was powerless to stop the mob. Amidst the confusion, the front door to the home was left open and the twins were exposed to the frigid night air. This was too much for the already sick Joseph Murdock, and five days later he died.

As I read this story, I was touched by the human side of Joseph Smith. He treated the responsibility to his family with the same feeling and passion that he did for his calling as a prophet of God. I wanted to capture in this painting the love Joseph had for his young family and the responsibility he felt to care for them. I found that love in a quiet moment where Joseph walks the floors while Emma sleeps.

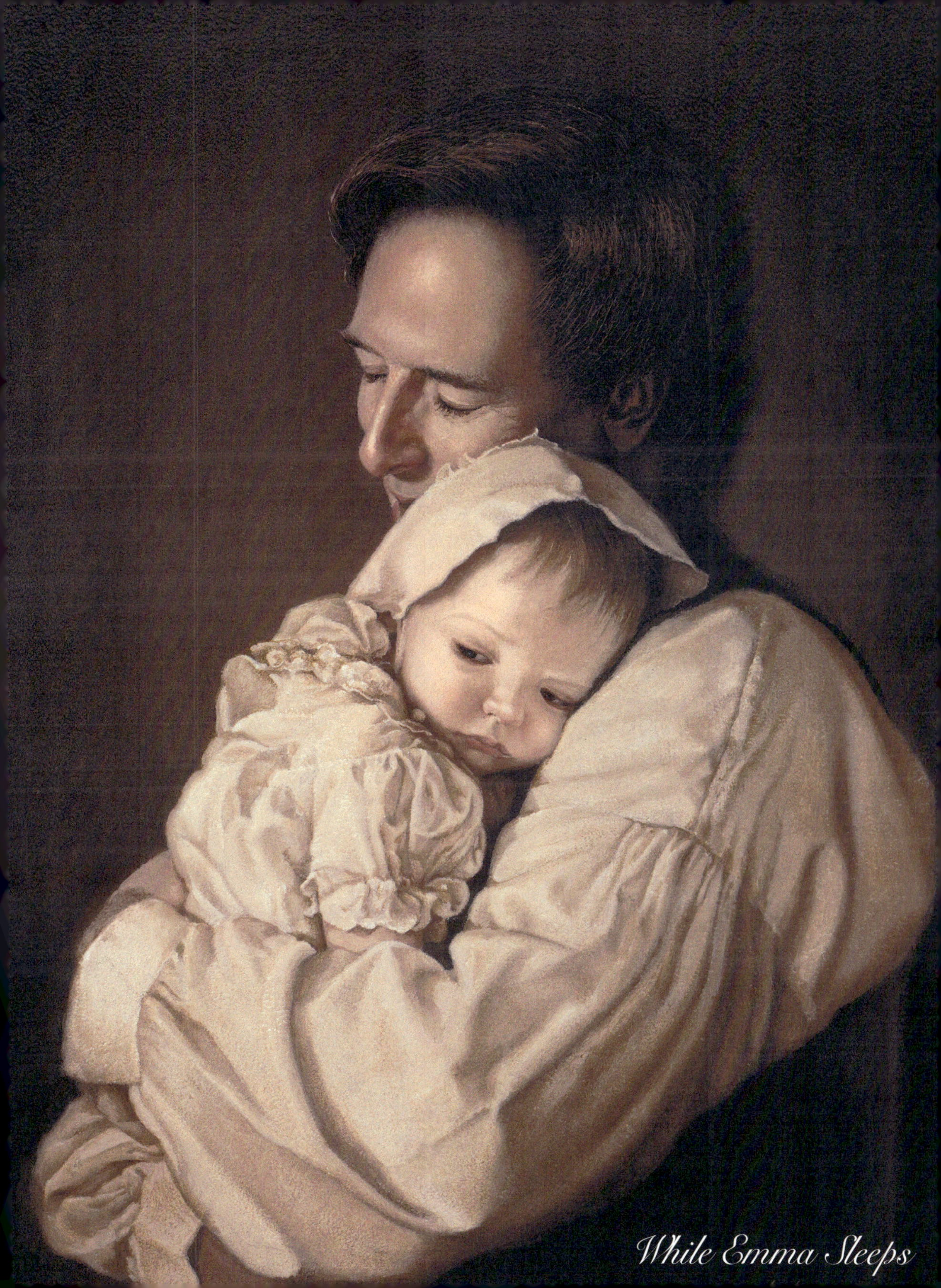

While Emma Sleeps

I remember after the birth of my first child when everyone had left and I was alone with my son for the first time. I looked at him lying on the bed and realized I was responsible for this new life. How could I teach him everything he needed? I was terrified.

I held him closely and the two of us cried. They were tears of fear and tears of joy, but most of all, they were tears of love. Looking into his little face, I made a promise to my God that I have spent my life trying to keep.

Was it different for Mary on that night in Bethlehem? Although Mary's calling as a mother was unlike any other, for she was chosen to raise the Messiah, like any first-time mother, she must have felt all the fear, all the joy, and all the love that comes with having a child. She must have marvelled at the overwhelming responsibility placed upon her. No mother can do this without guidance from above.

(Licensing shared with motion picture *The Young Messiah,* [2016].)

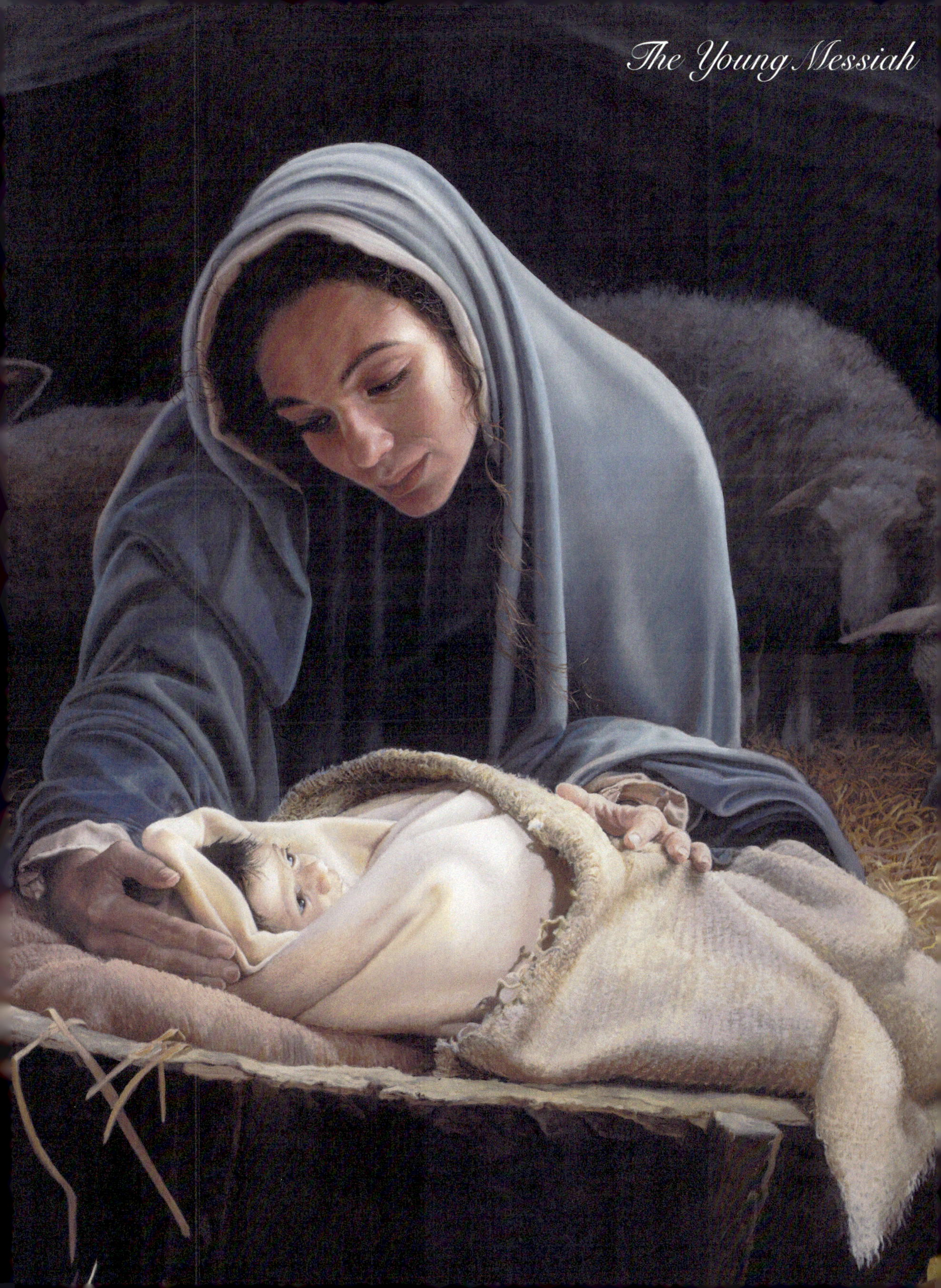
The Young Messiah

About the Author

Susan Easton Black was born and reared in Long Beach, California. She was the first woman to teach religion at BYU and the first woman to receive the Karl G. Maeser Distinguished Faculty Lecturer Award for her research and writing—the highest award given a professor at BYU. Susan is currently an emeritus professor of Church history and doctrine at Brigham Young University. Susan is the mother of three great sons. She enjoys writing, speaking, and being with her husband George.

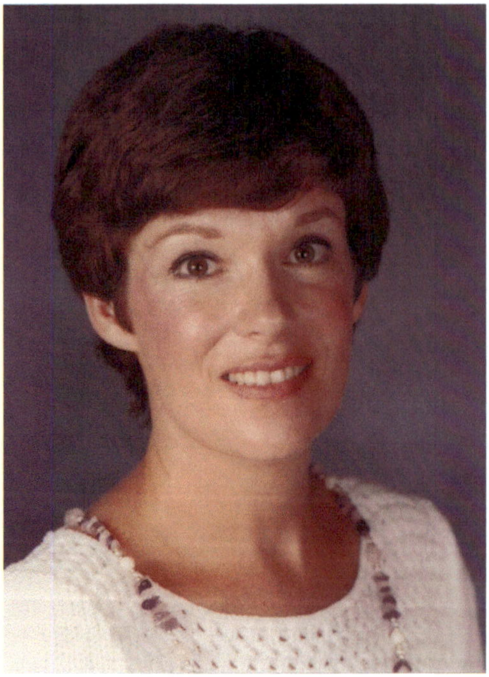